# Confusions

## Five interlinked one-act Plays

## Alan Ayckbourn

**Samuel French - London**
New York - Toronto - Hollywood

Please see page iv for further copyright information.

# CONFUSIONS

First presented by Michael Codron at the Apollo Theatre, London, on May 19th, 1976, with the following cast of characters:

## MOTHER FIGURE

| | |
|---|---|
| Lucy | Pauline Collins |
| Rosemary | Sheila Gish |
| Terry | Derek Fowlds |

## DRINKING COMPANION

| | |
|---|---|
| Harry | John Alderton |
| Paula | Pauline Collins |
| Bernice | Sheila Gish |
| Waiter | James Cossins |

## BETWEEN MOUTHFULS

| | |
|---|---|
| Waiter | John Alderton |
| Pearce | James Cossins |
| Mrs Pearce | Sheila Gish |
| Martin | Derek Fowlds |
| Polly | Pauline Collins |

## GOSFORTH'S FÊTE

| | |
|---|---|
| Mrs Pearce | Sheila Gish |
| Milly | Pauline Collins |
| Gosforth | John Alderton |
| Vicar | James Cossins |
| Stewart | Derek Fowlds |

## A TALK IN THE PARK

| | |
|---|---|
| Arthur | John Alderton |
| Beryl | Pauline Collins |
| Charles | James Cossins |
| Doreen | Sheila Gish |
| Ernest | Derek Fowlds |

The Plays directed by Alan Strachan
Settings by Alan Tagg

The action takes place in a living-room, a bar, a restaurant, a marquee and a park

Time—the present

## AUTHOR'S NOTE

These plays, although loosely linked, can of course be performed individually. When played together, it is recommended that they be presented in the order in which they appear here.

The entertainment was written originally for a cast of five (three male, two female). Obviously there are a variety of casting combinations which can be employed, depending on the actors available.

# MOTHER FIGURE

*Lucy's sitting-room*

*It is a suburban room, fairly untidy, with evidence of small children. There are two doors—one to the kitchen and back door, one to the bedrooms and front door*

*Lucy hurries in from the bedrooms on her way to the kitchen. She is untidy, unmade-up, in dressing-gown and slippers*

**Lucy** (*calling behind her*) Nicholas! Stay in your own bed and leave Sarah alone.

*The telephone rings*

> *Lucy goes out to the kitchen, returning at once with a glass of water*

All right, Jamie, darling. Mummy's coming with a dinkie . . . (*As she passes the telephone, she lifts the receiver off the rest and almost immediately replaces it*) Mummy's coming, Jamie, Mummy's coming.

> *Lucy goes off to the bedroom with the glass*

*The front door chimes sound. A pause, then they sound again*

> *Lucy returns from the bedrooms*

Sarah! You're a naughty, naughty girl. I told you not to play with Jamie's syrup. That's for Jamie's toothipegs . . .

*The door chimes sound again*

> *Lucy ignores these and goes off to the kitchen. She returns almost at once with a toilet roll, hauling off handfuls of it as she goes to perform some giant mopping-up operation*

Nicholas, if you're not in your bed by the time I come up, I shall smack your botty.

*There are two rings on the back door bell*

> *Lucy goes off to the bedroom*

*A pause*

*Rosemary, a rather frail, mousey-looking woman, comes in from the kitchen*

**Rosemary** (*calling timidly*) Woo-hoo!

*Lucy returns from the bedroom*

**Lucy** (*calling as before*) Now go to sleep. At once. (*Seeing Rosemary*) Oh.
**Rosemary** Hallo. I thought you must be in.
**Lucy** (*puzzled*) Hallo?
**Rosemary** I thought you were in.
**Lucy** Yes.
**Rosemary** You are.
**Lucy** Yes.
**Rosemary** Hallo.
**Lucy** Hallo. (*A slight pause*) Who are you?
**Rosemary** Next door.
**Lucy** What?
**Rosemary** From next door. Mrs Oates. Rosemary. Do you remember?
**Lucy** (*vaguely*) Oh, yes. Hallo.
**Rosemary** Hallo. I did ring both bells but nobody seemed ...
**Lucy** No. I don't take much notice of bells.
**Rosemary** Oh.
**Lucy** I've rather got my hands full.
**Rosemary** Oh yes. With the children, you mean? How are they?
**Lucy** Fine.
**Rosemary** All well?
**Lucy** Yes.
**Rosemary** Good. It's three you've got, isn't it?
**Lucy** Yes.
**Rosemary** Still, I expect it's time well spent.
**Lucy** I haven't much option.
**Rosemary** No.
**Lucy** Well.
**Rosemary** Oh, don't let me—if you want to get on ...
**Lucy** No.
**Rosemary** I mean, if you were going to bed.
**Lucy** Bed?
**Rosemary** (*indicating Lucy's attire*) Well ...
**Lucy** Oh, no. I didn't get dressed today, that's all.
**Rosemary** Oh. Not ill?
**Lucy** No.
**Rosemary** Oh.
**Lucy** I just wasn't going anywhere.
**Rosemary** Oh, well ...
**Lucy** I haven't been anywhere for weeks.
**Rosemary** That's a shame.
**Lucy** I don't think I've got dressed for weeks, either.

**Rosemary** Ah. No, well, I must say we haven't seen you. Not that we've been looking but we haven't seen you.

**Lucy** No. Do you want to sit down?

**Rosemary** Oh, thank you. Just for a minute.

**Lucy** If you can find somewhere. (*She moves the odd toy*)

**Rosemary** (*sitting*) Yes, we were wondering if you were alright, actually. My husband and I—Terry, that's my husband—he was remarking that we hadn't seen you for a bit.

**Lucy** No.

**Rosemary** We heard the children, of course. Not to complain of, mind you, but we heard them but we didn't see you.

**Lucy** No. (*She picks up various toys during the following and puts them in the play-pen*)

**Rosemary** Or your husband.

**Lucy** No.

**Rosemary** But then I said to Terry, if they need us they've only to ask. They know where we are. If they want to keep themselves to themselves, that's all right by us. I mean, that's why they put up that great big fence so they could keep themselves to themselves. And that's all right by us.

**Lucy** Good.

**Rosemary** And then ten minutes ago, we got this phone call.

**Lucy** Phone call?

**Rosemary** Yes. Terry answered it—that's my husband—and they say will you accept a transfer charge call from a public phone box in Middlesbrough and Terry says, hallo, that's funny, he says, who do we know in Middlesbrough and I said, not a soul and he says, well, that's funny, Terry says, well who is it? How do we know we know him? If we don't know him, we don't want to waste money talking to him but if we do, it might be an emergency and we won't sleep a wink. And the operator says, well suit yourself, take it or leave it, it's all the same to me. So we took it and it was your husband.

**Lucy** Harry?

**Rosemary** Harry, yes. Mr Compton.

**Lucy** What did he want?

**Rosemary** Well—you. He was worried. He's been ringing you for days. He's had the line checked but there's been no reply.

**Lucy** Oh.

**Rosemary** Has it not been ringing?

**Lucy** Possibly. I don't take much notice of bells. (*She goes to listen for the children*)

**Rosemary** Oh. Anyway, he sounded very worried. So I said I'd pop round and make sure. I took his number in case you wanted to . . .

*Lucy is clearly not listening*

Are you all right?

**Lucy** Yes, I was listening for Nicholas.

**Rosemary** Oh. That's the baby?

**Lucy** No.

**Rosemary** (*warmly*) Ah.

**Lucy** I'm sorry. I'm being very rude. It's just I haven't—spoken to anyone for days. My husband isn't home much.

**Rosemary** Oh, I quite understand. Would you like his number?

**Lucy** What?

**Rosemary** Your husband's telephone number in Middlesbrough. Would you like it? He said he'd hang on. It's from a hotel.

**Lucy** No.

**Rosemary** Oh.

**Lucy** Whatever he has to say to me, he can say to my face or not at all.

**Rosemary** Ah. (*Laying a slip of paper gingerly on the coffee-table*) Well, it's there.

**Lucy** Would you care for a drink or something?

**Rosemary** A drink? Oh—well—what's the time? Well—I don't know if I should. Half past—oh yes, well—why not? Yes, please. Why not? A little one.

**Lucy** Orange or lemon?

**Rosemary** I beg your pardon?

**Lucy** Orange juice or lemon juice? Or you can have milk.

**Rosemary** Oh, I see. I thought you meant . . .

**Lucy** Come on. Orange or lemon? I'm waiting.

**Rosemary** Is there a possibility of some coffee?

**Lucy** No.

**Rosemary** Oh.

**Lucy** It'll keep you awake. I'll get you an orange, it's better for you.

**Rosemary** Oh . . .

**Lucy** (*as she goes*) Sit still. Don't run around. I won't be a minute.

*Lucy goes out into the kitchen*

*Rosemary sits nervously. She rises after a second, looks guiltily towards the kitchen and sits again. The door chimes sound. Rosemary looks towards the kitchen. There is no sign of Lucy. The door chimes sound again. Rosemary gets up hesitantly*

**Rosemary** (*calling*) Mrs—er . . .

**Lucy** (*off, in the kitchen*) Wait, wait, wait! I'm coming . . .

*The door chimes sound again*

*Rosemary runs off to the front door. Lucy returns from the kitchen with a glass of orange juice*

Here we are, Rosemary, I . . . (*She looks round the empty room, annoyed. Calling*) Rosemary! It's on the table.

*Lucy puts the orange juice on the coffee-table and goes out to the kitchen again. Rosemary returns from the hall with Terry, a rather pudgy man in shirt sleeves*

**Rosemary** (*sotto voce*) Come in a minute.

**Terry** I'm watching the telly.

**Rosemary** Just for a minute.

**Terry** I wondered where you'd got to. I mean, all you had to do was give her the number . . .

**Rosemary** I want you to meet her. See what you think. I don't think she's well.

**Terry** How do you mean?

**Rosemary** She just seems . . .

**Terry** Is she ill?

**Rosemary** I don't know . . .

**Terry** Well, either she's ill or she isn't.

**Rosemary** Ssh.

*Lucy returns from the kitchen with a plate of biscuits*

**Lucy** Here we are now. (*Seeing Terry*) Oh.

**Terry** Evening.

**Lucy** Hallo.

**Rosemary** My husband.

**Lucy** Terry, isn't it?

**Terry** Yes.

**Lucy** That's a nice name, isn't it? (*Pointing to the sofa*) Sit down there then. Have you got your orange juice, Rosemary?

*Terry sits*

**Rosemary** Yes, thank you. (*She picks up the glass of orange juice and sits*)

**Terry** Orange juice?

**Rosemary** Yes.

**Terry** What are you doing drinking that?

**Rosemary** I like orange juice.

**Lucy** Now, here's some very special choccy bics but you mustn't eat them all. I'm going to trust you. (*She starts tidying up again*)

**Rosemary** (*still humouring her*) Lovely. (*She mouths "say something" to Terry*)

**Terry** Yes. Well, how are you keeping then—er, sorry, I'm forgetting. Lesley, isn't it?

**Lucy** Mrs Compton.

**Terry** Yes. Mrs Compton. How are you?

**Lucy** I'm very well, thank you, Terry. Nice of you to ask.

**Terry** And what about Har—Mr Compton?

**Lucy** Very well. When I last saw him. Rosemary dear, try not to make all that noise when you drink.

**Rosemary** Sorry.

**Terry** Yes, we were saying that your husband's job obviously takes him round and about a lot.

**Lucy** Yes. (*She starts folding nappies*)

**Terry** Doesn't get home as much as he'd like, I expect.

**Lucy** I've no idea.

**Terry** But then it takes all sorts. Take me, I'm home on the nose six o'clock every night. That's the way she wants it. Who am I . . . ? (*Pause*) Yes, I think I could quite envy your husband, sometimes. Getting about a bit. I mean, when you think about it, it's more natural. For a man. His natural way of life. Right back to the primitive. Woman stays in the cave, man the hunter goes off roving at will. Mind you, I think the idea originally was he went off hunting for food. Different sort of game these days, eh?

**Rosemary** (*hissing*) Terry!

**Terry** Be after something quite different these days, eh? (*He nods and winks*)

**Lucy** Now don't get silly, Terry.

**Terry** What? Ah—beg your pardon.

*A pause. Terry munches a biscuit. Rosemary sips her orange juice*

**Rosemary** Very pleasant orange juice.

**Lucy** Full of vitamin C.

**Terry** No, I didn't want to give you the wrong impression there. But seriously, I was saying to Rosie here, you can't put a man in a cage. You try to do that, you've lost him. See my point?

**Lucy** That can apply to women, too, surely?

**Rosemary** Yes, quite right.

**Terry** What do you mean, quite right?

**Rosemary** Well . . .

**Terry** You're happy enough at home, aren't you?

**Rosemary** Yes, but—yes—but . . .

**Terry** Well then, that's what I'm saying. You're the woman, you're happy enough at home looking after that. I'm the man, I have to be out and about.

**Rosemary** I don't know about that. You'd never go out at all unless I pushed you.

**Terry** What do you mean? I'm out all day.

**Rosemary** Only because you have to be. You wouldn't be if you didn't have to be. When you don't, you come in, sit down, watch the television and go to bed.

**Terry** I have to relax.

**Rosemary** You're always relaxing.

**Terry** Don't deny me relaxing.

**Rosemary** I don't.

**Terry** Yes, you do, you just said . . .

**Lucy** Now, don't quarrel. I won't have any quarrelling.

**Terry** Eh?

**Rosemary** Sorry.

**Lucy** Would you like an orange drink as well, Terry? Is that what it is?

**Terry** Er . . . Oh no—I don't go in for that sort of drink much, if you know what I mean. (*He winks, then reaches for a biscuit*) I'll have another one of these though, if you don't mind?

**Lucy** Just a minute, how many have you had?

**Terry** This is my second. It's only my second.

**Lucy** Well, that's all. No more after that. I'll get you some milk. You better have something that's good for you.

**Terry** (*half rising*) Oh no—thank you, not milk, no.

**Lucy** (*going to the kitchen*) Wait there. (*Seeing Terry has half risen*) And don't jump about while you're eating, Terry.

*Lucy goes out to the kitchen*

**Terry** You're right. She's odd.

**Rosemary** I said she was.

**Terry** No wonder he's gone off.

**Rosemary** Perhaps that's why she's odd.

**Terry** Why?

**Rosemary** Because he's gone off.

**Terry** Rubbish. And we'll have less of that, too, if you don't mind.

**Rosemary** What?

**Terry** All this business about me never going out of the house.

**Rosemary** It's true.

**Terry** It's not true and it makes me out to be some bloody idle loafer.

**Rosemary** All I said . . .

**Terry** And even if it is true, you have no business saying it in front of other people.

**Rosemary** Oh, honestly, Terry, you're so touchy. I can't say a thing right these days, can I?

**Terry** Very little. Now you come to mention it.

**Rosemary** Niggle, niggle, niggle. You keep on at me the whole time. I'm frightened to open my mouth these days. I don't know what's got into you lately. You're in a filthy mood from the moment you get up till you go to bed . . .

**Terry** What are you talking about?

**Rosemary** Grumbling and moaning . . .

**Terry** Oh, shut up.

**Rosemary** You're a misery to live with these days, you really are.

**Terry** I said, shut up.

**Rosemary** (*more quietly*) I wish to God you'd go off somewhere sometimes, I really do.

**Terry** Don't tempt me. I bloody feel like it occasionally, I can tell you.

**Rosemary** (*tearfully*) Oh, lovely . . .

**Terry** If you think I enjoy spending night after night sitting looking at you . . . (*He throws the biscuit down*) What am I eating these damn things for . . . you're mistaken. (*Thirsty from the biscuits, he grabs her orange juice glass and drains it in one*)

**Rosemary** That's mine, do you mind. (*She rises and stamps her foot*)

**Terry** Come on. Let's go. (*He jumps up*)

**Rosemary** That was my orange juice when you've quite finished.

*Lucy enters with a glass of milk*

**Lucy** Now what are you doing jumping about?

*Rosemary sits*

**Terry** We've got to be going, I'm sorry.

**Lucy** Not till you've finished. Sit down.

**Terry** Listen, I'm sorry we . . .

**Lucy** (*seeing Rosemary's distraught state*) What's the matter with Rosemary?

**Rosemary** (*sniffing*) Nothing . . .

**Terry** Nothing.

**Lucy** What have you been doing to her?

**Terry** Nothing.

**Lucy** Here's your milk.

**Terry** Thank you.

**Lucy** You don't deserve it.

**Terry** I don't want it.

**Lucy** Don't be tiresome.

**Terry** I hate the damned stuff.

**Lucy** I'm not going to waste my breath arguing with you, Terry. It's entirely up to you if you don't want to be big and strong.

**Terry** Now, look . . .

**Lucy** If you want to be a little weakling, that's up to you. Just don't come whining to me when all your nails and teeth fall out. Now then, Rosemary, let's see to you. (*She puts down the milk and picks up the biscuits*) Would you like a choccy biccy?

**Rosemary** No, thank you.

**Lucy** Come on, they're lovely choccy, look. Milk choccy . . .

**Rosemary** No, honestly.

**Terry** Rosie, are you coming or not?

**Lucy** Well, have a drink, then. Blow your nose and have a drink, that's a good girl. (*Seeing the glass*) Oh, it's all gone. You've drunk that quickly, haven't you?

**Rosemary** I didn't drink it. He did.

**Lucy** What?

**Rosemary** He drank it.

**Lucy** Terry, did you drink her orange juice?

**Terry** Look, there's a programme I want to watch . . .

**Lucy** Did you drink Rosemary's orange juice?

**Terry** Look, good night . . .

**Rosemary** Yes, he did.

**Lucy** Well, I think that's really mean.

**Rosemary** He just takes anything he wants.

**Lucy** Really mean.

**Rosemary** Never thinks of asking.

**Terry** I'm going.

**Lucy** Not before you've apologized to Rosemary.

**Terry**  Good night.

*Terry goes out*

**Lucy** (*calling after him*)  And don't you dare come back until you're ready to apologize. (*To Rosemary*) Never mind him. Let him go. He'll be back.
**Rosemary**  That's the way to talk to him.
**Lucy**  What?
**Rosemary**  That's the way he ought to be talked to more often.
**Lucy**  I'm sorry. I won't have that sort of behaviour. Not from anyone.
**Rosemary**  He'll sulk now. For days.
**Lucy**  Well, let him. It doesn't worry us, does it?
**Rosemary**  No. It's just sometimes—things get on top of you—and then he comes back at night—and he starts on at me and I . . . (*She cries*) Oh dear—I'm so sorry—I didn't mean to . . .
**Lucy** (*cooing*)  Come on now. Come on . . .
**Rosemary**  I've never done this. I'm sorry . . .
**Lucy**  That's all right. There, there.
**Rosemary**  I'm sorry. (*She continues to weep*)
**Lucy**  Look who's watching you.
**Rosemary**  Who?
**Lucy** (*picking up a doll*)  Mr Poddle. Mr Poddle's watching you. (*She holds up the doll*) You don't want Mr Poddle to see you crying, do you? Do you?
**Rosemary** (*lamely*)  No . . .
**Lucy**  Do we, Mr Poddle? (*She shakes Mr Poddle's head*) No, he says, no. Stop crying, Rosie. (*She nods Mr Poddle's head*) Stop crying, Rosie. Yes—yes.

*Rosemary gives an embarrassed giggle*

That's better. Was that a little laugh, Mr Poddle? Was that a little laugh?

*Lucy wiggles Mr Poddle about, bringing him close up to Rosemary's face and taking him away again*

Was that a little laugh? Was that a little laugh? Was that a little laugh?

*Rosemary giggles uncontrollably*

*Terry enters from the hall and stands amazed*

**Terry**  Er . . .

*Lucy and Rosemary become aware of him*

Er—I've locked myself out.
**Lucy**  Have you come back to apologize?
**Terry**  You got the key, Rosie?

**Rosemary** Yes.

**Terry** Let's have it then.

**Lucy** Not until you apologize.

**Terry** Look, I'm not apologizing to anyone. I just want the key. To get back into my own house, if you don't mind. Now, come on.

**Rosemary** (*producing the key from her bag*) Here.

**Lucy** Rosemary, don't you dare give it to him.

**Terry** Eh?

**Rosemary** What?

**Lucy** Not until he apologizes.

**Terry** Rosie, give me the key.

**Lucy** No, Rosemary. I'll take it. Give it to me.

**Terry** Rosie.

**Lucy** Rosemary.

**Rosemary** (*torn*) Er . . .

**Lucy** (*very fiercely*) Rosemary, will you give me that key at once.

*Rosemary gives Lucy the key. Terry regards Lucy*

**Terry** Would you mind most awfully giving me the key to my own front door?

**Lucy** Certainly.

**Terry** Thank you so much.

**Lucy** Just as soon as you've apologized to Rosemary.

**Terry** I've said, I'm not apologizing to anyone.

**Lucy** Then you're not having the key.

**Terry** Now listen, I've got a day's work to do tomorrow. I'm damned if I'm going to start playing games with some frustrated nutter . . .

**Rosemary** Terry . . .

**Lucy** Take no notice of him, Rosemary, he's just showing off.

**Terry** Are you going to give me that key or not?

**Lucy** Not until you apologize.

**Terry** All right. I'll have to come and take it off you, won't I?

**Lucy** You try. You just dare try, my boy.

**Terry** All right. (*He moves towards Lucy*)

**Rosemary** Terry . . .

**Lucy** Just you try and see what happens.

**Terry** (*halted by her tone; uncertainly*) I'm not joking.

**Lucy** Neither am I.

**Terry** Look, I don't want to . . . Just give me the key, there's a good . . .

**Lucy** Not until you apologize to Rosemary.

**Terry** Oh, for the love of . . . All right (*To Rosemary*) Sorry.

**Lucy** Say it nicely.

**Terry** I'm very sorry, Rosie. Now give us the key, for God's sake.

**Lucy** When you've drunk your milk. Sit down and drink your milk.

**Terry** Oh, blimey . . . (*He sits*)

**Lucy** That's better.

**Terry** I hate milk.

**Lucy** Drink it up.

*Terry scowls and picks up the glass. Rosemary, unseen by Lucy, sticks her tongue out at him. Terry bangs down his glass and moves as if to hit her*

Terry!

**Terry** She stuck her tongue out at me.

**Lucy** Sit still.

**Terry** But she . . .

**Lucy** Sit!

*Terry sits scowling. Rosemary smirks at him smugly*

(*Seeing her*) And don't do that, Rosemary. If the wind changes, you'll get stuck like it. And sit up straight and don't slouch.

*Rosemary does so*

**Terry** (*taking a sip of the milk*) This is horrible.

*Silence. He takes another sip*

It's warm.

*Silence. Another sip*

**Terry** There's a football international on television, you know.

**Lucy** Not until you've drunk that up, there isn't. Come on, Rosemary. Help Terry to drink it. "Georgie Porgie Pudding and Pie, Kissed the girls and . . . ?"

**Rosemary** "Made them cry."

**Lucy** Good.

**Rosemary** } "When the boys came out to play, Georgie Porgie } (*Speaking*
**Lucy** } ran away." } *together*)

**Terry** (*finishing his glass with a giant swallow*) All gone. (*He wipes his mouth*)

**Lucy** Good boy.

**Terry** Can I have the key now, please?

**Lucy** Here you are.

*Terry goes to take it*

What do you say?

**Terry** Thank you.

**Lucy** All right. Off you go, both of you.

**Rosemary** (*kissing her on the cheek*) Night night.

**Lucy** Night night, dear. Night night, Terry.

**Terry** (*kissing Lucy likewise*) Night night.

**Lucy** Sleep tight.

**Terry** Hope the bugs don't bite.

**Lucy** Hold Rosemary's hand, Terry.

*Rosemary and Terry hold hands*

See her home safely.

**Terry** Night.

**Rosemary** Night.
**Lucy** Night night.

*Terry and Rosemary go off hand in hand*

*Lucy blows kisses*

(*With a sigh*) Blooming kids. Honestly.

*The telephone rings. Lucy, as she passes it, picks it up and replaces it as before. As she does so, the Lights fade to a single spot in a call-box. Harry is there, with the receiver in his hand*

**Harry** Oh, blast, not again. Hallo—hallo—oh, damn and blast. (*He jiggles the receiver*) Operator? Operator? Hallo—hallo . . . Operator, there must be a fault on this line. . . . The line I have been trying unsuccessfully to dial. . . . Yes—six-four-one-nine. I mean, this is quite unforgivable. This is the third time I have reported it and I am still quite unable to make contact with my wife. . . . Yes, well, thank you for your sympathy. Let's try a little action, shall we? Because I'm going to take this to the top. . . . Yes, top. . . . What? . . . No—T for Toffee, O for Orange. . . . Oh, forget it. (*He rings off*) Give me strength.

*Harry moves out of the box. As he does so, the Lights come up to full, and the set has now changed to—*

# DRINKING COMPANION

*A three-star hotel bar*

*Discreet muzak is being played. Paula, a girl in her twenties, sits alone at a table, her coat and handbag beside her. On the table are her own vodka and tonic, and an unfinished whisky and soda. Harry, a man in his forties, returns and sits beside her*

**Harry** Sorry. Sorry about that. Not getting lonely, are you?
**Paula** No.
**Harry** After all that, would you believe it, couldn't get through. I get the ringing tone then it just cuts off like that. I think there's a fault on the line. Cheers. (*He drinks*)
**Paula** Who were you trying to phone?
**Harry** (*evasively*) Oh, just—family. You know.
**Paula** You're wife?
**Harry** Yes . . .
**Paula** You're married?
**Harry** Yes.
**Paula** Have you got any children?
**Harry** Yes, yes . . . Can I get you another?
**Paula** Oh, well, just one more.
**Harry** (*calling*) Waiter. (*To Paula*) Same again, is it? Vodka and tonic?
**Paula** Lovely.

*The Waiter appears*

**Harry** Ah, Waiter. We want the same again, here, please. Vodka and tonic and scotch and soda.
**Waiter** Right, sir. (*He turns to go*)
**Harry** You'd better make them large ones.
**Paula** Oh, well . . .
**Waiter** Large whisky, large vodka, sir.

*The Waiter goes*

**Harry** You were saying you were just up here for a couple of days.
**Paula** That's right. We go back tomorrow.
**Harry** Extraordinary, you know. I was walking through Mason's this morning, on the ground floor, and I saw you two there, you and your friend—what's her name?
**Paula** Bernice.
**Harry** Bernice. Pretty name. Paula and Bernice—lovely names—and I

thought to myself, hallo, they don't belong here. They look right out of place. Two lovely personalities like yours just don't go together with Mason's. No, I thought to myself—they're from London I wouldn't mind betting. Up for a visit. Promoting that—what was it you were selling?

**Paula** Perfume.

**Harry** And I said to myself, I wouldn't mind betting, Harry, that what's more those will be staying at the "Crown". And then it just so happens I look out of the door of the bar here and lo and behold—there you are, standing in the foyer.

**Paula** Coincidence.

**Harry** Not really. There's only one place to stay in this town. Well, you've got the "Wheatsheaf" or the "Black Horse" but they're not to be recommended, take it from me. When you're here, always plunk for the "Crown". How have your demonstrations been going? All right?

**Paula** Oh, extremely well. We're just on this short promotion tour for their new brand, you see.

**Harry** Is that the delicious fragrance I can smell even now?

**Paula** Oh yes, I think I've got some on.

**Harry** Very very nice. Very very nice indeed.

**Paula** It's proving very popular. It's exotic without being cloying and can be worn equally well day or night.

**Harry** You get commission on it, do you?

**Paula** Yes. They pay very well.

**Harry** Well, you need some inducement to come up here. What do you think of the place?

**Paula** It's all right, I suppose.

**Harry** Dreadful. Dead and alive place. Goes to bed at six o'clock at night, you know. No word of a lie. I've walked through the main street here, the main street mark you, at seven-thirty p.m. on a Saturday night and there has not been one single soul.

**Paula** Good gracious.

**Harry** Not one single soul. Empty. Deserted.

**Paula** You often here?

**Harry** Once every two months or so. Just a sales check really. I mean, my firm doesn't treat this area very seriously. Consumer demand is negligible. Our only stockist is Mason's. We're fairly exclusive, you see. That's why I was in there today going over our sales with Mr Molyneux. He's their chief chap, you know. Not at all bad when you get to know him but I must say our sales were very disappointing.

**Paula** We sold a lot of perfume.

**Harry** Yes, well, you'd be alright with that. But our line, you see, well, I suppose you'd call us *haute couture*—high fashion anyway. Cut above the average. Not much call for it up here. Predominantly working class, you see. Very small market.

*The muzak fades out*

**Paula** There's not many young people. We noticed that.

**Harry** No. There's not many girls, like, well, like yourself for instance. Now, you'd look very good in some of our stuff. Very good indeed.

**Paula** Really?

**Harry** Yes. (*Staring at her*) Orange. Tangerine shades. That's your colour.

**Paula** Is it?

**Harry** Definitely. You ought to go in for tangerine shades, take my tip. I'm good at that, you know. I can match a woman to her colour like that. Almost do it automatically these days.

**Paula** Really?

**Harry** You're what I call a modern girl, you see. You need modern shades, modern styling. Have you ever modelled by any chance?

**Paula** No, I don't think I've quite the . . .

**Harry** Oh, come on, come on. We don't always want them like sticks of celery, you know. Bit of shape never did a girl any harm. Some of our styles would really suit you.

*The Waiter returns with the drinks*

Ah. Thank you. Vodka and tonic there.

**Waiter** Thank you, sir. Thank you, madam.

**Harry** Could you charge it to Room two-four-nine, please?

**Waiter** Two-four-nine. Very good, sir. (*He waits*)

**Harry** Oh, just a second, just a second. (*Fumbling in his pocket and producing a handful of silver*) Here.

**Waiter** Oh. That's very good of you, sir, thank you.

*The Waiter leaves*

**Harry** Cheers. No, put it this way. In my particular line I've got to be able to look at a woman and say yes, you'd look good in so and so. Straightaway.

**Paula** Yes, I can see that.

**Harry** The same with you. No difference. Straightaway.

**Paula** Yes.

*A slight pause*

**Harry** You married, by any chance?

**Paula** No. Not likely.

**Harry** What, don't you fancy it?

**Paula** Not at the moment.

**Harry** Very sensible. Take my word. Steer clear.

**Paula** Don't let your wife hear you say that.

**Harry** Well, you know what I mean. Always envy what you haven't got, don't you?

**Paula** Oh yes?

**Harry** Freedom. I miss that. In the old days if I'd walked in here, say, and I'd met someone attractive—like I'm meeting you for instance . . .

**Paula** (*laughing*) Me?

**Harry** No—joking apart—seriously—well, you know, you could just allow things to happen.

**Paula** What sort of things?

**Harry** Well, that depends on the girl, doesn't it?

**Paula** Oh, I see.

**Harry** Cheers. Got a boyfriend, have you?

**Paula** One or two.

**Harry** Bet you have.

**Paula** Nothing serious. Nobody special.

**Harry** Playing the field?

**Paula** More or less.

**Harry** Why not? At your age. What are you? Twenty-one, I'd say at a guess.

**Paula** Some hope.

**Harry** What, younger than that?

**Paula** Twenty-five.

**Harry** Twenty-five? Get on with you. Thirty-seven.

**Paula** Oh yes?

**Harry** Thirty-seven. I don't look thirty-seven, do I?

**Paula** No.

**Harry** Not bad for thirty-seven. Ready for another one?

**Paula** No. I've hardly started this.

**Harry** No, in my opinion you young people today are doing the most sensible thing you can do. I mean, I know there's a lot of people of my generation that you could call narrow minded but I think it's just marvellous that a girl like you today, she can take her time, look around, get to know a few men for herself—you know, even sleep with them if she feels like it—and no hang-ups. Marvellous.

**Paula** What makes you think I do that?

**Harry** No, what I'm saying is . . .

**Paula** I don't go sleeping around, you know.

**Harry** No, that's not what I was saying. What I was saying . . .

**Paula** I don't fancy doing that.

**Harry** No, no, quite. But if you did happen to fancy it, there'd be nothing to stop you. That's what I was saying.

**Paula** Possibly.

**Harry** I mean, that's all I was saying. Cheers.

**Paula** Where do you live, then?

**Harry** Me? London. Well, just outside. Luton really.

**Paula** Oh.

**Harry** And you?

**Paula** Shepherd's Bush.

**Harry** Oh, really? I know Shepherd's Bush very well. Very pleasant. Parts of it.

**Paula** Yes, it is.

*Pause*

**Harry** No, to get back to our previous conversation. Look at it this way.

We're two adult people. This is now, the present, today. We can sit here and talk about—well, whatever we care to talk about—let's say for the sake of argument—sex—without feeling embarrassed. Now I think that's a tremendous step forward. When you think of the past.

*Pause*

I mean, I'm able to sit here, enjoy a drink in the middle of a public hotel, talking to a very, very attractive girl, if I may say so, and not feel in the least embarrassed. And she can do the same. You can do the same.

**Paula** It's a nice hotel.

**Harry** Not bad. Not marvellous, but not bad. Cheers.

*Pause*

The bedrooms are good. Have you got a nice room?

**Paula** Fine.

**Harry** Single?

**Paula** No. We've got a twin.

**Harry** We?

**Paula** Me and Bernice.

**Harry** Oh yes. That's your friend?

**Paula** Yes.

**Harry** I've got a double. I mean, it's just me in there but I've got a double. I can't bear small rooms, you see. Well, the firm's paying so why not. Besides, better to be prepared, isn't it?

**Paula** How do you mean?

**Harry** (*laughing*) No, it's a particularly nice room, two-four-nine. Always try and book it when I'm here. *En suite* bathroom, all the trimmings. Here, look—(*he produces his room key*)—two-four-nine, you see. Room two-four-nine. If you should come back here again, take my tip, try and get two-four-nine. I think it is the quietest room they've got. Not round the front, you see, it's round the side.

**Paula** That's good.

**Harry** Where are you two, then?

**Paula** Eh?

**Harry** What number?

**Paula** Oh, do you know, I can't remember offhand.

**Harry** Well, I hope your friend does. Otherwise you'll be wandering round all night, won't you? Probably finish up in two-four-nine if I'm lucky. (*He laughs*) Cheers.

*Pause*

Tell you what, are you likely to be paying a return visit any time?

**Paula** What, up here?

**Harry** Yes, you'll probably be coming back sometime, won't you?

**Paula** Shouldn't think so.

**Harry** You never know. When they see how much perfume you've sold, they'll probably send you straight back here to sell some more.

**Paula** It's only a temporary job.

**Harry** Well, if they should by any chance, you're bound to want to stay here again, aren't you? Nowhere else.

**Paula** I shouldn't think we'll . . .

**Harry** Well, what I was going to say is, would you like to have a quick look at two-four-nine? See if it'd suit you. You know, just in case you do come back.

**Paula** Oh no.

**Harry** No, I mean just literally pop upstairs, stick your nose round the door, see what you think.

**Paula** No, I couldn't really . . .

**Harry** Hang on, hang on, even better. Do you know what I've got up there? I've just remembered, I've got a bottle of whisky. Do you like whisky?

**Paula** No, I hate it.

**Harry** Of course, what am I saying, you're a vodka girl, aren't you? Tell you what, even better, I'll have a word with this chap, get him to send us up a bottle of vodka. I'll drink the scotch, you drink the vodka, we'll have a party.

**Paula** No, honestly, it's very nice of you but I'd rather not.

**Harry** Well, I mean, suit yourself. I mean, nothing like that. We can go to your room if you'd rather.

**Paula** No, thank you very much all the same.

**Harry** Ah, well. Not to bother. Just thought you'd care to have a look. Ready for another one?

**Paula** No, honestly, you've been very kind but I really have to be . . . (*Breaking off as she sees someone in the saloon bar*) Oh, here she is. Bernice!

**Harry** Hallo, it's your friend, isn't it?

*Bernice enters. She is a few years older than Paula*

Hallo there. (*He rises*)

**Bernice** You said in the foyer.

**Paula** I'm sorry. I met this gentleman, you see. Bernice, this is—er, Harry, isn't it?

**Harry** Harry Compton, how do you do?

**Bernice** (*without really taking him in*) How do you do? (*To Paula*) You said you'd be in the foyer.

**Paula** Well, we're only sitting here just round the corner.

**Bernice** I didn't see you just round the corner though, did I?

**Harry** Now, can I get you a drink, Bernice?

**Bernice** Yes, I'll have a gin and tonic, thank you.

**Harry** Gin and tonic for Bernice. Another vodka for Paula.

**Paula** No, no.

**Harry** (*calling*) Waiter! Can I take your coat, Bernice?

**Bernice** No, I'll keep it on, thank you. I've been out there half an hour, you know.

**Paula** I'm sorry.

**Bernice** Well ...

**Harry** Now, now, now. Mustn't quarrel, girls. Waiter.

**Bernice** (*sitting*) My God, this place is a dump.

**Harry** (*sitting again by Paula*) Just what we were saying, wasn't it, Paula?
After six o'clock, absolutely dead.

**Bernice** And it was freezing in that shop, what's more.

**Harry** Yes, it's very bad that. I mean there's no excuse for that. Waiter!
Where the hell's he gone to? Hang on, I'll get them myself, it's quicker.
Just wait there, girls, I won't be a second. Bernice's thirsty, we can't
have that.

*Harry goes off to the bar*

**Bernice** Who's your friend?

**Paula** Oh, you know. He was the one hanging around the counter this
morning. The one with all the funny remarks.

**Bernice** Oh, yes, that's right. That's him. How did you finish up with
him?

**Paula** Because you were late and he caught me standing there on my own
in the foyer.

**Bernice** I was not late. What's he like?

**Paula** Well, you know ...

**Bernice** Let's go then, shall we?

**Paula** He's buying us a drink now.

**Bernice** So? We don't want to get stuck with him, do we?

**Paula** Well, we might as well have the drink now.

**Bernice** Alright. Then we'll tell him we've got to get back to our hotel.
Tell him you're expecting a phone call or something.

**Paula** That's no good. He thinks we're staying here.

**Bernice** How did he come to think that?

**Paula** I don't know, he just did. If we tell him we're at the "Wheatsheaf"
he'll only follow us there.

**Bernice** He won't. (*She produces a scent spray*)

**Paula** He will.

**Bernice** Why should he?

**Paula** Because he's one of those. We've only been talking five minutes and
he's been trying to get me up to his bedroom.

**Bernice** I don't know why you wanted to come to this place anyway. (*She
sprays behind her ears*)

**Paula** Well, Simon said it was good.

**Bernice** You should know better than to trust Simon. (*She sprays behind
her knees*)

*Harry returns with drinks*

**Harry** Here we are then, girls. (*Handing them out*) That's the gin, that's
the vodka.

**Bernice** Oh, that's a very big one.

**Harry** Well. Saves jumping up and down, doesn't it? Now then. Finished your argument? Cheers.

**Paula** Cheers.

**Harry** Been out looking at the town, have you?

**Bernice** Beg your pardon?

**Harry** Saw you'd got your coat on. Thought you might have been out.

**Bernice** Oh, yes I went for a walk.

**Harry** Not much of a place for walks, is it?

**Bernice** No.

**Harry** Well, this is the life, isn't it? When I woke up this morning and I knew I was due to come over here, my heart sank I don't mind saying. Then what happens? I finish up with two beautiful girls for company. Just goes to show.

**Paula** Yes.

**Harry** Paula and I, we've been chatting away, haven't we, Paula?

**Paula** Yes.

**Harry** Right, now. Let's see how I do with Bernice, eh, Paula?

**Bernice** What?

**Harry** Now, looking at Bernice—I immediately think of blue. Am I right? You look good in blue, am I right?

**Bernice** Me?

**Harry** That's your best colour. Best for you, if you're interested, blue.

**Bernice** No, I never wear blue.

**Paula** You've got that blue trouser suit.

**Bernice** I never wear blue. I hate it.

**Harry** Well, I could be wrong. It has been known, but it's unusual. You have another look at yourself in blue. See if I'm not right. I'm not talking about royal blue, not a dark blue—more of a pale blue. We've got this dress at the moment, it's in this new material, man-made fibre with ten per cent wool—crease-resistant—it's literally a dress you can roll in a ball, jump on it if you like, give it a shake, put it on, good as new. Now this is a really beautiful blue. A sort of ice blue I suppose you'd call it. Knee length, not a long one. It's got a top rather like you've got on now and I'm not joking, looking at your colouring, Bernice, it would really set that off. Can you see that, Paula, Bernice in blue?

**Paula** Yes, nice.

**Harry** She'd look really fantastic. When I saw you this morning at the counter there in amongst all your bottles and perfumes and things, I thought straightaway, that is the girl who could really wear that dress.

**Bernice** I wouldn't be seen dead in blue.

**Harry** Ah well. Cheers. No, as I say, I never thought I'd be spending this evening with two gorgeous girls.

**Bernice** You never know your luck, do you.

**Harry** Quite right, Bernice, many a true word. Never know your luck. Well. How are we three going to spend this evening?

**Bernice** Well, we're . . .

**Harry** Now, now. Plenty of time. Enjoy your drink first, then we'll decide.

The night is young, as they say. So are we. Well, in my case, young in heart. (*He laughs*)

**Paula** I don't think we'll be wanting to do very much this evening, actually.

**Harry** All right, fair enough. Let's just stay here then. Fine by me. Have a bite of dinner later.

**Bernice** Oh no.

**Harry** It's very good, the restaurant here, you know.

**Paula** Oh no.

**Harry** On me. On me. I don't often have the pleasure.

**Bernice** I don't think actually either of us are very hungry, thank you.

**Harry** Oh, come on, you've got to eat, you've got to eat. Keep up your strength. No, seriously, I would consider it a great honour. A great honour. Besides, there's nothing worse than eating alone, is there? Be nice if, just for once—the life I lead, I seem to spend my life eating alone.

**Paula** Well, when you're at home you don't . . .

**Harry** Ah, well. On those occasions, on those rare occasions . . . Matter of fact, to be frank, I'm not often there. I mean, I don't want to start boring you by talking about myself particularly but, well—let's just say I'm not very often at home. Enough said? Enough said. Cheers. (*Pause*) I mean, don't get me wrong. My wife and I, we're not separated, anything like that. It's just—well, to be perfectly honest she's a lot happier if I'm not at home too much. You might say, we no longer see eye to eye. If you follow my meaning. She's got very strong views on certain matters and, er—well there you are. I mean, I'm—as I was saying only a minute ago to Paula here—I'm by nature—easy going. However, it takes all sorts as they say. It so happens my wife is one of those people who considers that these sort of things cannot be forgiven or forgotten—particularly not forgotten—ever. No matter. No matter how much you may talk to her or apologize to her about it. She's not a woman to take sorry for an answer. So there you are. I live there. On occasions. That's about all. But it's not life. I don't call that life. (*Pause*) Anyway, enough of my problems. (*Pause*) The point is this, if my wife were sitting here now with us all, she would have no claim over me whatsoever. Nor, let's be perfectly honest, would I have on her. Washout. Finish. Waiter, we'll have the same again, please.

*The Waiter approaches*

**Bernice** No, thank you very much.

**Paula** No. Harry, Harry . . .

**Harry** Waiter! Same again here.

**Bernice** No, thank you very much. No more, Waiter.

**Harry** Waiter, we want three more of the same.

**Paula** No, honestly, Harry . . .

**Harry** Three more, Waiter, we'll argue it out later.

**Waiter** Three more, sir.

*The Waiter departs*

**Bernice** I don't want any more.

**Harry** Come on, that's only your first.

**Bernice** That's all I want.

**Harry** You've got to catch up with me and Paula, for God's sake.

**Bernice** I don't have to at all.

**Paula** It's very kind of you.

**Harry** Well, he's bringing them now, it's too late. You needn't worry, it's on me. On me. I mean, I'm not a big drinker either, you know. Don't get me wrong. I'm not hooked on it. I can go for weeks without a drink, you know, if I have to. Doesn't bother me in the least. But, for God's sake, if I get the chance of sitting here with two simply stunning-looking creatures the like of which I have never set eyes upon before, believe you me—well, I think it calls for a drink. I don't drink at home, you know. Never drink at home.

**Bernice** You're never there.

**Harry** I only drink socially. I only drink to be sociable. No, never been my problem, drink. I've got other problems but drink's not one of them. Thank God. And I do very sincerely thank God. I won't go into my other problems, I don't want to shock you. (*He laughs*) I mean, today, you won't believe that today, I was drinking all lunchtime with a colleague of mine, an old friend, a dear old friend I hadn't seen for a very long time. We had a few together over lunch, I won't deny that and I happened to be in here again when they opened the bar this evening. And I haven't even got a thick head. Would you believe that? Incredible, isn't it?

*The Waiter arrives with drinks*

Ah. Thank you very much, Waiter. Good man, good man. Room two-four-nine.

**Waiter** Two-four-nine, sir. Will that be all, sir?

**Harry** For the time being, thank you very much. (*As the Waiter goes, he calls him back*) Oh, Waiter. Here, here—just a sec. (*Fumbling in his pocket and producing a pound note*) Here's for yourself.

**Waiter** Oh, that's very kind of you. Thank you very much, sir.

**Harry** Have one yourself.

**Waiter** Very kind indeed, sir.

*The Waiter goes*

**Harry** Take care of them. They'll take care of you. Cheers.

**Bernice** (*not touching her drink*) Cheers.

**Harry** No, I'll tell you both something now. I'll be absolutely honest with you—now, I don't want you to be shocked because the last thing I want to do in this world to you two lovely girls is to shock you but I have to say, you are both of you—now I'm not in any way trying to get off with you, anything like that, you are two of the most amazingly startlingly sexy girls I have ever seen in my life. Now that's no—no— sort of kidding at all. I want you to believe that.

**Paula** Thank you very much.

**Harry** No, no, Paula my darling, I want to hear you say you believe that. Will you say very clearly, I believe that.

**Paula** Yes, we do.

**Harry** You do believe that, don't you?

**Paula** Yes.

*Bernice gives her a "come on" look*

Harry, Bernice has got to meet her uncle at the station

**Harry** Just a minute, let me finish . . .

**Paula** She's got to meet her uncle at the station, you see, Harry. The train's due in a few minutes.

**Harry** No, well I'll get you down to the station, my darling, don't you worry about that. I'll get you a taxi.

**Paula** No, Harry . . .

**Harry** I'll buy you a taxi.

**Paula** We have to go, Harry.

**Harry** No. Listen, listen, Paula, Paula—Bernice. Listen. This is not in any way an advance, it's not anything like that, please believe that. I mean, I respect you far too much, you see. I respect you as ladies. Look, you see this . . . (*Holding up his room key*) This is a key, right? The key to my room, two-four-nine, which is a very, very nice room, believe me. Now, I'm going to put this key down here in the middle of the table, like that. Now, I'm going to leave it there. I'm not going to try and embarrass you, you see, but it's there. If you want to pick it up, it's there. Entirely up to you. Can't say fairer than that.

*Bernice rises*

Where are you going?

**Bernice** We have to go.

*Paula tries to rise. Harry pushes her down*

**Harry** Paula, there's the key, you see.

**Paula** Yes, but you'll need it, Harry.

**Harry** No, I'll get another one. They have another one at the desk. This is for you.

**Bernice** Come on.

**Harry** If you want it, there it is.

**Paula** Thank you very much, Harry.

**Harry** Two-four-nine. If you want it, come and get it.

**Paula** Thank you, Harry. We have to meet her uncle, you see.

**Bernice** Paula, are you coming?

**Paula** Yes, I'm coming. (*She rises*)

**Harry** (*catching Paula's wrist*) Just a minute, just a minute. Waiter,
   Waiter.
**Paula** Wait.

   *The Waiter arrives*

**Harry** Waiter.
**Waiter** Yes, sir?
**Harry** I wonder, Waiter, if you'd do me a favour. These two enchanting
   young ladies want to go to—where is it?—the railway station—to meet
   their uncle. Could you arrange them a taxi, do you think?
**Waiter** The hall porter will get you a taxi, sir.
**Harry** Ah, well. Would you mind asking him very nicely.
**Waiter** I'm sorry, sir, I'm not allowed to leave the bar.
**Harry** Oh, for crying out loud.
**Paula** It doesn't matter, Harry, don't bother.
**Bernice** Are you coming?
**Harry** What's the matter with this place?
**Paula** We'll walk, Harry, we can walk.
**Harry** You're not walking. I'm not having you walking, not on your own.
   I'm going to get you a taxi.
**Bernice** (*moving in*) We don't want a taxi, thank you.
**Harry** (*pushing her aside*) Wait there. (*Confidentially*) Paula.
**Paula** What?
**Harry** (*pushing the room key into her hand*) Here. You keep this. You
   understand. It's up to you. It's entirely up to you. I want you to know
   that. No strings. No strings at all.
**Paula** Thank you.
**Harry** (*blundering off*) I won't be a moment. Waiter, I'm relying on you
   to keep an eye on these magnificent girls.
**Waiter** I'll do that, sir.
**Harry** Wait there.

   *Harry goes through the saloon bar*

**Bernice** Oh my God, I thought we'd never get rid of him.
**Paula** Awful when they get like that.
**Bernice** Thought you'd have learnt better by now. We'd better go quick.
**Paula** We can't. He's just out there.
**Bernice** (*to the Waiter*) Is there another way out, please?
**Waiter** Yes, just through there, madam. There's a side door just through
   to your left.
**Bernice** Thank you. Right, come on, let's go.
**Paula** Good night.
**Waiter** Good night to you, madam.

*The girls start to move off by the side door*

   Oh, madam, excuse me—you won't forget to leave the key, will you?

**Paula** Oh. Nearly forgot. (*She hands him the key*) Would you mind?
**Waiter** Not at all, madam. Good night.

*Paula and Bernice go*

*The Waiter slips the key into his pocket and starts to clear the empties, as the Lights fade to a Black-out*

# BETWEEN MOUTHFULS

*A hotel dining-room*

*Two tables are set apart, each with two chairs. Between them a service table. An IN and OUT door from the kitchens. The main entrance for Guests. The discreet clatter of knives and forks from other invisible diners. The Waiter is finishing arranging his two tables. He wanders over and leans against the service table. At length, Donald Pearce enters, a middle-aged businessman*

**Waiter** (*approaching him*) Good evening, sir.

**Pearce** Good evening. I have a table for two reserved in the name of Pearce.

**Waiter** Table for two, sir. Did you make a reservation, sir?

**Pearce** Yes, I've just said I did.

**Waiter** Very good, sir. (*He consults the reservations book on the service table*) What name was it, sir?

**Pearce** Pearce. I've just this minute said so.

**Waiter** Pearce—with a P, I presume?—ah, yes, sir. (*Indicating the table nearer the door*) Would this one over here suit you, sir?

**Pearce** No, I don't think it would. I think I'd prefer this one over here.

**Waiter** Oh, just as you like, sir.

*The Waiter leads Pearce over to the table and holds the chair for Pearce, who sits, his back to the rest of the room*

**Pearce** Thank you.

**Waiter** Just yourself is it, sir?

**Pearce** No.

**Waiter** Ah. Someone will be joining you, will they, sir?

**Pearce** Yes, indeed. That's really rather why I reserved a table for two.

**Waiter** Right, sir.

*The Waiter goes to the service table to collect menus*

> *Emma Pearce enters, same age as Pearce, worried and tense. She catches sight of her husband and moves across to join him*

*The Waiter hurries across to help her with her chair*

**Pearce** Oh, there you are.

**Waiter** Good evening, madam.

**Mrs Pearce** (*sitting*) Thank you. (*To Pearce*) You might have waited for me.

**Pearce** I had absolutely no idea where you'd got to.

**Mrs Pearce** You know perfectly well where I was.

**Waiter** (*handing her a menu*) Thank you, madam.

**Mrs Pearce** I told you.

**Waiter** Thank you, sir.

**Pearce** Thank you.

**Mrs Pearce** Oh lord. I suppose I've got to read through all this. (*She fumbles in her bag*)

**Waiter** Would you, madam, or yourself care for a drink before your meal, sir?

**Pearce** No, we wouldn't, thank you.

**Mrs Pearce** Oh no, I haven't brought them.

**Pearce** We may have some wine.

**Waiter** Right, sir.

**Mrs Pearce** That's that. I haven't brought them. (*She takes out a cigarette*)

**Pearce** What?

**Mrs Pearce** My reading glasses. I've left them at home.

**Pearce** I suppose that means I've got to read it to you.

*The Waiter lights Mrs Pearce's cigarette*

**Mrs Pearce** Unless you want me to guess.

**Pearce** (*to the Waiter*) Would you bring us an ashtray, please.

**Waiter** Yes, sir.

**Pearce** Why the hell you can't keep your glasses permanently in your handbag . . .

*The Waiter moves away. As he does so, Pearce's voice fades out. Throughout we hear only that dialogue that the Waiter himself hears when within earshot. Whether or not the Waiter registers the content of what he is hearing apart from remarks directly addressed to him, he never betrays. Pearce continues speaking, but we can no longer hear him. The Waiter fetches the ashtray from the service table, dusts it, and returns to Pearce's table*

**Mrs Pearce** (*fading up*) . . . this afternoon whilst I was reading and I forgot them, that's all.

**Pearce** All right, all right, all right.

**Mrs Pearce** (*to the Waiter*) Thank you.

**Pearce** And we'll have the wine list as well.

**Waiter** Wine list. Yes, sir.

**Pearce** Now then, are you listening? Here we go. (*Reading*) Hors d'oeuvres from our trolley, grapefruit cocktail . . . (*He fades out*)

*The Waiter returns to the service table for the wine list*

*Polly and Martin enter, a younger couple*

**Waiter** Good evening, sir. Good evening, madam. Just the two of you, is there?

**Martin** That's right.

**Waiter** Have you a reservation, sir?

**Martin** No, we haven't.

**Waiter** Just a moment, sir. (*He consults the book*)

**Polly** I hope there's going to be room.

**Martin** (*looking round the restaurant*) There'll be room. (*Catching sight of the Pearces*) God, look who's here.

**Polly** Where?

**Martin** Over there, look. Donald Pearce and his wife.

**Polly** Oh.

**Martin** Better go and say hallo.

**Polly** No, don't do that.

**Martin** What?

**Polly** Let's go somewhere else.

**Martin** What?

**Polly** They'll only feel they'll have to ask us to join them. Let's go somewhere else.

**Martin** I'm not going somewhere else.

**Polly** They haven't seen us yet. Quick . . .

**Martin** I'm not going somewhere else. What's the matter with you?

**Polly** I just don't feel like talking to them.

**Martin** Why not?

**Polly** Not now.

**Waiter** Sorry to keep you, sir. Would this table here be all right, sir?

**Martin** (*as they follow him to the other table*) You can't expect me to cut my boss dead in a restaurant.

**Polly** We'll have to pretend we haven't seen them.

**Martin** It's obvious we've seen them.

**Polly** Why? They haven't seen us. We could leave now.

*The Waiter holds the chair for Polly*

**Martin** I'm not leaving now. (*He sits. To the Waiter*) Thank you. (*To Polly*) What's got into you?

**Polly** Nothing. (*She sits*)

**Waiter** Excuse me, sir.

**Martin** I mean, I thought you always got on with them.

**Polly** They're all right.

**Waiter** Excuse me, sir.

**Martin** You've always been quite happy to talk to them in the past.

**Waiter** Would you care for a drink before your meal, sir?

**Martin** You used to be perfectly happy . . . (*To the Waiter*) No, thank you —perfectly happy to go round when they invited us.

**Polly** Not tonight. I don't feel like sitting down . . . (*She fades out*)

*The Waiter returns to the service table and picks up the wine list. He moves to the Pearces' table with it*

**Pearce** (*fading up*) . . . Dover sole meuniere. Lobster thermidor. Lobster americaine brackets when in season. Scampi—all sorts of scampi—grilled halibut . . . (*He fades out*)

*The Waiter has slipped the wine list down beside Pearce's elbow and departed. He returns to his service table, takes up two menus and crosses to Martin's table*

**Polly** . . . seen you for three weeks. I'd rather like it if we were just on our own.

**Martin** I'm not the one who went away.

**Polly** All the same . . .

**Martin** I mean, you're the one who went off on holiday. I didn't go off on holiday.

**Polly** You could have done. (*Taking her menu*) Thank you.

**Martin** I couldn't, I told you. Old Pearce there—(*taking his menu*)—thank you—old Pearce there landed me with enough work to last me a year.

**Polly** That wasn't my fault, Martin . . .

**Martin** I'm not saying it was. I was merely explaining why . . .

*The Waiter departs. He edges towards the Pearces' table with his order pad*

**Pearce** . . . grilled pork chops, tournedos à la Crowne—whatever that may be—steak diane, grilled fillet steak brackets when available. Rump steak—Garni . . .

*The Waiter withdraws and leans against the service table, waiting. After a moment, he moves again to Martin's table to see if any decision has been made there*

**Martin** . . . book a holiday at a time when you know I'm going to be very busy.

**Polly** Because if I waited for you not to be busy I'd never get a holiday at all.

**Martin** Come on, darling. This chap wants us to order.

**Waiter** No hurry, sir, no hurry.

**Polly** I mean, it was either a case of my taking a holiday on my own or not having a . . .

*The Waiter wanders back to the Pearces*

**Pearce** . . . roast Aylesbury duckling with orange sauce. Roast spring chicken with stuffing. Roast turkey with cranberry sauce . . .

*The Waiter withdraws. Martin signals for the Waiter. The Waiter moves to Martin's table*

**Polly** . . . enjoy going on holiday on my own.

**Martin** Waiter, what's the Soup of the Day?

**Waiter** (*checking over Martin's shoulder*) Er—minestrone, sir.

**Martin** (*unenthusiastically*) Oh.

*Martin and Polly ponder their menus. The Waiter hovers*

How was the trip back?

**Polly** Not bad. Had to be at the airport at seven this morning. We got to Heathrow at ten . . .

**Martin** Sorry I couldn't meet you.
**Polly** I didn't expect you to.
**Martin** Our sales meeting went on till lunchtime.

*Pearce signals and mimes   Waiter*

**Waiter** Yes, sir?

*The Waiter moves across from Martin's table to Pearce's*

**Pearce** Waiter, what is the Soup of the Day?
**Waiter** Minestrone, sir.
**Pearce** Oh.

*Pause*

**Waiter** Do you wish to order now, sir?
**Mrs Pearce** Do you do Eggs Benedict?
**Waiter** (*doubtfully; looking over Pearce's shoulder*) Eggs Benedict, madam . . .
**Pearce** I should imagine that if they did  Eggs Benedict, they'd have put Eggs Benedict on the menu.
**Waiter** I don't think we do, madam.
**Mrs Pearce** I was only asking.
**Pearce** I mean, I read you the menu very distinctly. I didn't read out Eggs Benedict, did I?
**Mrs Pearce** I don't know.
**Pearce** But I've only just this minute finished reading it to you.
**Mrs Pearce** I don't know, I wasn't listening.
**Pearce** (*taking a deep breath*) I think we need a few more minutes to decide, Waiter.
**Waiter** Very good, sir.
**Pearce** I suppose you want me to read it to you all over again . . .

*The Waiter hovers back near Martin and Polly*

**Polly** . . . marvellous the whole time. Baking hot. And it's a beautiful island.
**Martin** (*uninterestedly*) Yes. Sounds it. (*Seeing the Waiter*) Ah. Now then. So far we've got one pâté—one smoked trout. And you were . . . ?
**Waiter** (*writing*) Pâté maison—smoked trout.
**Polly** Is the lobster fresh?
**Waiter** Oh yes, madam. I can recommend it.
**Polly** Then I'll have Thermidor with a green salad.
**Martin** Poulet estragon for me.
**Waiter** Poulet estragon—thermidor. Would you care to see the wine list, sir?
**Martin** Might as well. My wife has just returned from the sunny Mediterranean. She's probably got the taste after three weeks.
**Waiter** Very nice, too, madam. Excuse me a moment, sir.

*The Waiter moves across again to the Pearces*

**Mrs Pearce** ... the moment you come back, you start.
**Pearce** I'm not starting again. I was merely saying ... (*Seeing the Waiter*) Yes?
**Waiter** I just wondered if you were ready with your order yet, sir.
**Pearce** No indeed, we are not ready with our order yet. We will let you know when we are.
**Waiter** Very good, sir.
**Mrs Pearce** Every single time you come back from somewhere, you're absolutely ...

*The Waiter collects the wine list from the service table*

**Martin** ... it was your idea.
**Polly** I didn't know they were going to be here, did I?
**Martin** It was your idea we came out.
**Polly** Since the children were away, I thought it would be nice.
**Martin** It was a lovely idea. Enjoy it.
**Polly** Yes, but I didn't know they were going to be here, did I ...
**Pearce** (*calling*) Waiter!

*The Waiter returns to Pearce*

**Waiter** Sir?
**Pearce** You will be pleased to hear that we have at last decided. Pencil at the ready. Here we go. One potted shrimps—one grapefruit cocktail and if it has a maraschino cherry on it, we don't want it. One Dover sole meuniere off the bone—one rump steak, just this side of medium rare ...
**Waiter** (*scribbling furiously*) Just a minute, sir—Dover sole off the bone—rump steak, medium rare ... Have you decided on a wine, sir?
**Pearce** Oh—yes. (*He opens the list*) White? Emma? White, do you want white?
**Mrs Pearce** I don't mind either way. I only want half a glass.
**Pearce** Well, just say red or white?
**Mrs Pearce** I honestly don't mind. (*She looks out front*)
**Pearce** Red, then.

*Mrs Pearce turns sharply and glares at him*

Ah, now. What have you got in the Italian line?
**Waiter** I think they're at the back here, sir. The wine waiter's not on at the moment, otherwise ...
**Pearce** Ah yes, here we are, Italian. We had a very very reasonable one at the hotel where we stayed.
**Mrs Pearce** I thought you went there to work.
**Pearce** I did go there to work. I had to stop occasionally. Now then.
**Mrs Pearce** My husband's been overworking in Italy, poor thing ...
**Pearce** No, you don't seem to have it.
**Mrs Pearce** I don't know how you managed to work in all that blazing sunshine.
**Pearce** A bottle of this one here, the—er—one-oh-four.

**Waiter** Oh right, sir. The—er—one-oh-four. Yes, sir.

**Mrs Pearce** How on earth did you manage to cope for three whole weeks . . . ?

*The Waiter goes out through to the kitchens and after a second, returns. He takes up some cutlery, places it on a tray and crosses to Martin's table*

**Martin** . . . last six months are beginning to move. Somebody up there seems to have our interests at heart, anyway.

**Waiter** Smoked trout, madam?

**Martin** No, that's me—and not before time, as far as I'm concerned. Old Pearce was back this afternoon, full of the joys of spring, anyway. I don't know what he got up to in Rome but he seems to have had a good time of it.

*The Waiter exchanges some of Polly's and Martin's cutlery, replacing it with a fish knife and fork*

**Polly** I thought he went on business.

**Martin** I can't believe it took him three weeks to get a contract signed. I know the Italians are difficult . . . mind you, I think if I was married to Emma Pearce, I'd chase off to Rome.

**Polly** Don't stare.

**Martin** It's all right, he's got his back to us. And she's as blind as a bat. No, he probably had some little Italian señora lined up there. He always likes to mix his business with a bit of . . .

*The Waiter goes to Pearce's table*

**Waiter** Potted shrimps, sir?

**Pearce** Thank you.

**Waiter** And a steak for madam?

**Pearce** No, that's for me as well.

*A pause while the Waiter exchanges cutlery, replacing Mrs Pearce's with a fish knife and fork, and Pearce's with an outer fish knife and fork and a steak knife*

**Mrs Pearce** Well, I'm sorry, I don't believe you.

**Pearce** That's up to you. (*Pause*) That's what I was doing.

**Mrs Pearce** I'm sorry, I think you're a liar.

*The Waiter crosses to Martin and Polly*

**Martin** . . . and the problem was to re-allocate staff work schedules so that everyone was guaranteed at least one day off in three whilst guaranteeing normal production.

**Polly** Yes.

**Waiter** Excuse me, sir.

**Martin** Which was one hell of a problem. Yes?

**Waiter** Have you chosen a wine, sir?

**Martin** (*picking up the wine list*) Oh yes—you see, as soon as you say, lost men off the assembly section, you had to insure you had sufficient manpower to tide you over the entire three-day period without any noticeable shrinkage in labour effectiveness.

**Polly** Martin, he's waiting to know what wine.

**Martin** Oh yes. Do you do a carafe?

**Waiter** Yes, sir.

**Martin** A carafe of white. Not too sweet.

**Waiter** Carafe of the white, sir

**Martin** Anyway, we managed it. We put in the report and Donald Pearce is over the moon. I mean, he only had time to glance at it this afternoon but . . .

*The Waiter goes into the kitchens*

*The Pearces sit in silence. Martin chatters on to Polly*

*The Waiter returns with the Pearces' first courses, grapefruit cocktail, potted shrimps, plate of toast. He crosses to Pearce's table*

**Waiter** Grapefruit cocktail, madam?

**Mrs Pearce** Thank you.

**Waiter** Potted shrimps, sir.

**Pearce** Thank you.

**Mrs Pearce** I'm sorry, I think you're lying.

**Waiter** Beg your pardon, madam? Oh, I'm sorry, madam, I beg your pardon. Toast is there, sir.

*The Waiter returns to the kitchens*

*The Pearces eat, Martin continues to talk*

*The Waiter returns with Martin's and Polly's first courses. He goes to their table*

**Martin** . . . so in the end I did the only thing possible. I took on entire responsibility for the whole A, D and J project. Took on both jobs. Did the lot myself.

**Polly** Yes, I know, you told me this before, Martin.

*The Waiter serves her with pâté*

Thank you.

**Martin** When did I tell you? (*He leans forward over the table*)

*The Waiter tries unsuccessfully to slip the plate under Martin's hands*

**Polly** I've only been away three weeks, you know.

**Martin** What time are we picking up the kids?

**Polly** I told Gran we'd be there in time for lunch.

**Martin** Ah well, end of peace and quiet. (*He leans back*)

*The Waiter quickly slides Martin's plate into place*

　　Thank you.

**Polly** Did you miss them?

**Martin** I honestly haven't had a moment to miss anyone, love. Not even you.

**Polly** I missed them dreadfully.

**Waiter** (*fiddling at the table*) Toast is just there, madam.

**Polly** Thank you

**Martin** Oh, did I tell you, Graham Shotter finally got that job in Glasgow.

**Polly** Oh, did he . . .

*The Waiter goes to the kitchen, returning with both the carafe and Pearce's wine. He puts the carafe down on the service table, wipes the bottle, shakes it upside down, then takes it to Pearce's table and holds it out for his inspection*

**Waiter** Sir. The one-oh-four, sir.

**Pearce** Oh yes. (*He reads the label very carefully, muttering all the words to himself including the name of the shippers*) Righto, yes.

**Waiter** Thank you, sir.

*The Waiter produces a cork-screw from his pocket and starts to open the bottle by their table*

**Pearce** Did you get someone in to look at that radiator in the bedroom?

**Mrs Pearce** They said they'd come on Tuesday.

**Pearce** Oh.

**Mrs Pearce** He said it sounded as if it needed a new part.

**Pearce** That's out.

*The Waiter pulls out the cork with a "pop"*

　　I'm not paying for a new part. I'm not wasting money on that.

**Mrs Pearce** Just on holidays. (*She lights another cigarette*)

*The Waiter pours a little wine into Pearce's glass*

**Pearce** Are you deliberately trying to annoy me this evening?

**Waiter** Would you care to try it, sir?

**Pearce** Oh . . . (*He sips his glass*) Bit on the chill side. It'll do. Go ahead.

**Waiter** Thank you, sir.

*The Waiter starts to pour wine for Mrs Pearce*

**Mrs Pearce** That's enough, thank you.

**Waiter** Thank you, madam.

**Pearce** Are you eating that or just leaving it?

**Mrs Pearce** Leaving it.

*The Waiter pours Pearce the rest of his glass and puts the bottle on the table*

**Waiter** I'll leave it here, sir. Finished, madam?
**Mrs Pearce** Yes, thank you.
**Waiter** Was it all right for you, madam?
**Mrs Pearce** Beautiful. I'm just not very hungry.
**Waiter** (*removing her plate*) Thank you, madam.
**Pearce** I don't see any point in ordering food if you're not going to eat it . . .

*The Waiter returns to the service table, picks up the carafe of wine and crosses to Martin and Polly's table*

**Polly** I just think it's a terrific cheek, that's all.
**Martin** No, honestly, love, it isn't really I—thank you—

*The Waiter starts to pour wine for Polly. She picks up her glass while he is still pouring*

The quality of the wife is frightfully important. If you've got a top executive virtually responsible for what?—two or three hundred men sometimes—it's vitally important that he's married to the right woman.
**Polly** Why?
**Martin** Well, that he has a stable relationship. That she's suddenly not going to walk out on him.

*The Waiter picks up Martin's glass and fills it, so that Martin cannot touch it until he has finished pouring*

**Polly** She's going to take no part in his work, is she?
**Martin** Well, hardly, no.
**Polly** Then I think the firm ought to mind its own bloody business, I'm sorry . . .

*The Waiter moves away, Pearce finishes. The Waiter moves in to take his plate*

**Mrs Pearce** I said, who is she?
**Pearce** Who is who?
**Mrs Pearce** Who is she?

*Pearce opens his mouth to reply then becomes aware of the waiter. The Waiter takes away his plate and puts it on the service table. He sees Polly and Martin have finished and goes to remove their plates*

**Polly** . . . what I'm saying is, that as far as I'm concerned, you could be manufacturing—marmalade. You spend all day in the office, you work at home most of the night, you never talk to the children and I don't even know half the time what it is that you're doing.
**Martin** Look, darling, you wouldn't understand if I told you . . .

*The Waiter takes the empty plates to the kitchen*

*Pearce and Mrs Pearce are having a short, terse conversation. Martin talks agitatedly. Polly looks slightly desperate*

*The Waiter returns with the Pearces' second course: rump steak for him, Dover sole for her, and vegetables. He goes to their table*

**Pearce** I don't think this is quite the occasion for this sort of conversation, do you?

**Mrs Pearce** I can't think of any better time.

**Pearce** In a public restaurant.

**Mrs Pearce** Why not?

**Waiter** Dover sole, madam.

**Mrs Pearce** Thank you.

**Pearce** I don't see any point in causing a scene . . .

**Mrs Pearce** I am not causing a scene. I asked you a perfectly normal question. Who is this woman?

**Waiter** Rump steak, sir.

**Pearce** What does it matter?

**Mrs Pearce** Because I want to know.

**Pearce** Who said there was anyone, anyway?

**Mrs Pearce** Oh, come along, darling, I am not a fool. I am not a bloody fool.

**Pearce** Would you mind lowering your voice.

**Mrs Pearce** I will not lower my voice.

**Waiter** Runner beans, madam?

**Mrs Pearce** No, thank you.

**Waiter** Carrots, madam?

**Mrs Pearce** No, thank you. I want nothing else.

**Waiter** No potatoes either, madam?

**Mrs Pearce** (*shrilly*) Nothing else.

**Waiter** Very good, madam. (*He moves round to Pearce*)

**Pearce** (*to Mrs Pearce, fiercely*) Could you kindly try and control yourself.

**Waiter** Runner beans for you, sir?

**Pearce** (*snarling at him*) Yes please.

**Mrs Pearce** Well, I'll tell you one thing, darling, if I ever get my hands on the little whore, I'll wring her neck.

**Pearce** Do you mind, do you mind.

**Waiter** Carrots, sir?

**Pearce** Yes.

**Mrs Pearce** You can tell the little bitch that from me.

**Waiter** Potatoes, sir?

**Pearce** No. No potatoes. Nothing else.

**Waiter** Very good, sir.

**Pearce** Nothing else, at all.

**Waiter** Right, sir.

*The Waiter moves away and returns to the kitchens*

*Both tables are in a fair state of animation*

*The Waiter returns with Polly's and Martin's main courses: lobster, chicken, salad dressing, salad, vegetables. He moves to their table*

**Polly** . . . that's what it boils down to. I'm not in the slightest bit interested in your work and you don't give a damn what I'm up to. There we are. We haven't one thing in common.

**Martin** Oh, come on, I don't know.

*The Waiter serves Polly's lobster*

**Polly** Thank you.

**Martin** I'm interested in what you're up to.

**Polly** Really?

**Martin** Of course . . .

**Polly** Nonsense.

**Martin** It's not nonsense at all.

**Waiter** (*serving*) Poulet estragon, sir.

**Polly** These last three weeks I was away, were you the slightest bit interested in where I was?

**Martin** I know where you were.

**Polly** Do you?

**Martin** You were in—wherever it is—Majorca.

**Polly** I was not in Majorca, darling, as it happens. I was in Rome.

**Waiter** Vegetables, sir?

**Martin** Er—just carrots. Rome? What were you doing in Rome?

**Polly** I was with Donald Pearce.

**Martin** Donald Pearce—that's fine, thank you—what were you doing with Donald Pearce?

**Polly** I spent three weeks with Donald Pearce in a hotel in Rome.

**Martin** My God. (*He puts his head in his hands on the table*)

**Waiter** Potatoes, sir?

**Martin** Oh my God.

**Waiter** (*bending right down to speak to Martin*) Excuse me, sir.

**Polly** (*to the Waiter*) No, he doesn't.

**Waiter** Oh, right, madam.

**Polly** (*to Martin*) I'm sorry.

**Waiter** Sorry, madam?

**Polly** Nothing.

**Waiter** Oh, sorry, madam. Green salad.

**Martin** Oh my God.

**Polly** Thank you.

**Waiter** French dressing, madam?

**Polly** Yes, just a little.

**Martin** How could you do it?

**Polly** I don't know. I'm sorry. I felt—I don't know . . .

**Martin** You realize what you've done?

**Polly** It's not important, darling, it's all over. That's why I told you.

**Martin** It may be all over for you. What happens when she finds out?

**Polly** Who?

**Martin** Emma Pearce. You realize what's going to happen to me.

**Polly** What?

**Martin** I'll be out on my ear. As soon as Emma Pearce gets wind of—oh, damn it. If you were going to choose someone why the hell did it have to be Donald Pearce? That's it, don't you see? That's the end of everything. The end of my prospects of promotion. I shall probably be forced to resign.

**Polly** Is that what's worrying you?

**Martin** Of course it's what's worrying me.

**Waiter** Is that sufficient for you, madam?

**Polly** Oh, for crying out loud, I can't believe it—I just can't believe it. (*She stands, pushing back her chair*)

**Martin** Where are you going?

**Polly** Don't you care anything for me? Nothing at all?

**Martin** Where are you going?

**Polly** I'm going to be physically sick.

*Polly storms out*

**Waiter** Was everything all right for madam, sir?

**Martin** Yes, it was fine, fine. Thank you very much

**Waiter** Thank you, sir.

*The Waiter moves away and crosses to the Pearces' table with the intention of topping up the wine glasses, trying not to be noticed*

**Pearce** For the last time, will you pull yourself together.

**Mrs Pearce** I'll kill her when I see her, I'll kill her.

**Pearce** Don't be so stupid. (*Seeing the Waiter, sharply*) What do you want?

**Waiter** I was—just going to pour some more wine, sir.

**Pearce** We can do that ourselves. Go away.

**Waiter** Just as you like, sir. (*He starts to go*)

**Mrs Pearce** Waiter.

**Waiter** Madam?

**Mrs Pearce** (*indicating her plate*) You can take this away.

**Waiter** Have you finished, madam?

**Mrs Pearce** Yes, it was quite delicious, thank you very much. (*She gets up*) Excuse me.

**Waiter** Was everything all right, madam?

**Mrs Pearce** Perfectly. It's just I'm afraid I'm unable to enjoy a meal with a man who turns out to be a deceitful, lecherous liar.

*Mrs Pearce flips Pearce's plate into his lap. Pearce leaps up*

*Mrs Pearce goes out of the restaurant hurriedly, blowing her nose. She passes by Martin without seeing him*

*Martin, sitting stunned, does not see her*

**Pearce** (*dabbing at his trousers with his napkin*) Oh, for the love of mike.

**Waiter** I'll get a cloth, sir. Just a minute.

**Pearce** Look at this, look at this. Where's the Gents? I'll have to mop up.

*Martin rises*

**Waiter** Just through here, sir. I'll show you.

*The Waiter leads Pearce to the door past Martin's table. Martin has risen*

**Pearce** Damn fool thing to do. What a damn . . . (*He bumps into Martin*) Excuse me, I—good God, hallo, Chalmers.

**Martin** Oh, hallo, Mr Pearce.

**Pearce** I didn't know you were here. Excuse me, I've just had a bit of a mishap.

**Martin** Oh, good heavens, yes.

**Pearce** Having a night out, are you?

**Martin** Yes, yes, that's right.

**Pearce** So are we. Well, have to unwind once in a while, don't you?

**Martin** Rather, rather . . .

**Pearce** Are you still eating, or are you . . . ?

**Martin** No, I was just . . .

**Pearce** Well, I'll tell you what. I've just got to have a quick mop up in the Gents. Won't be a second. Then—fancy a quick brandy in the bar?

**Martin** Oh, that would be very nice indeed, Mr Pearce.

**Pearce** Just a quick one . . . (*To the Waiter, who is still mopping at his trouser*) All right, that'll do, Waiter, thank you. Could you bring the bill through to the bar, please.

**Waiter** Yes, of course, sir.

**Pearce** Oh, and you can put them all on to one if you like.

**Martin** Oh, that's most generous of you, sir.

**Pearce** Not at all, not at all. I think after all that stalwart work you've done on that report I probably owe you a meal, don't I?

**Martin** Oh, I don't know about that . . .

*The Waiter moves out of earshot. Pearce claps Martin on the back. The Waiter starts to clear the Pearces' table*

*Pearce and Martin leave the restaurant, Pearce with his hand on Martin's shoulder, both laughing and talking animatedly*

*The Waiter looks out front, as—*

*the* CURTAIN *falls*

# GOSFORTH'S FÊTE

*A tea tent*

*One long trestle table, the odd bench or collapsible chair. In one corner near one of the entrances, a jerry-rigged rather large valve-type amplifier with wires leading from it to outside. Another entrance at the other end of the table*

*Milly, a fresh-faced pink woman, staggers in with a box of teacups. She is wearing an overall-coat. She dumps the cups on the table. She attempts to assess the number in the box without removing them. She is involved with this when Emma Pearce comes in through the other entrance. She is now smartly turned out in a feather hat, light raincoat, white gloves with smart matching bag and shoes*

**Mrs Pearce** Excuse me.
**Milly** I'm sorry, I'm afraid we're not serving teas for another two hours. Can I help you at all?
**Mrs Pearce** Well, I'm Emma Pearce.
**Milly** Em—oh golly. Councillor Mrs Pearce.
**Mrs Pearce** That's right.
**Milly** Oh. Golly. Um. Well. Has nobody met you?
**Mrs Pearce** No. I saw one or two people. They seemed rather busy.
**Milly** Oh, yes . . .
**Mrs Pearce** I parked just in the lane there. Is that alright?
**Milly** Fine. I should think. I'm afraid we're all a bit behindhand.
**Mrs Pearce** Yes. Well, Mr—er—Gosfirth . . .
**Milly** Gosforth, yes . . .
**Mrs Pearce** He did say in his letter two-fifteen.
**Milly** He should be about—somewhere. He was. I'm Milly Carter.

*They shake hands*

**Mrs Pearce** How do you do.
**Milly** It's very nice of you to come.
**Mrs Pearce** Quite all right.
**Milly** Is your husband any better?
**Mrs Pearce** Better?
**Milly** Yes. Hasn't he been ill?
**Mrs Pearce** No.
**Milly** Oh. I thought that's why he couldn't come. Sorry.
**Mrs Pearce** No. It's just he had some business to see to. He couldn't get away. At the last minute.

**Milly** Oh, I see.

**Mrs Pearce** So you'll have to make do with me, I'm afraid.

**Milly** Yes . . . Oh, no. Not at all. We all tremendously appreciate your being here. Really. Super. Really.

**Mrs Pearce** Thank you.

**Milly** And it's for a jolly good cause.

**Mrs Pearce** Yes, indeed.

**Milly** I mean, it's just what this place needs—a new village hall. Did you pass the old one on your way here? You probably did.

**Mrs Pearce** Was that the building on the . . .?

**Milly** Yes. Just along the lane there. I mean, frankly it's an eyesore. It was put up during the war. All corrugated iron. If you're holding a meeting and it rains, you might as well save your breath.

**Mrs Pearce** Oh dear. The weather looks a little threatening today.

**Milly** Yes. I do hope it doesn't rain. I mean, we can house quite a lot of our activities in the marquee over there—or even in this tea tent if the worst came to the worst, but there's things like Mr Stokes's Wolf Cubs' P.T. display—you couldn't fit that in here for instance.

**Mrs Pearce** Were those Wolf Cubs, all those little boys out there in gym vests?

**Milly** Yes. Were they behaving themselves?

**Mrs Pearce** They were throwing stones at a caravan. I told them to stop it.

**Milly** Oh lord, good for you. They won't take a blind bit of notice. They're all little horrors. Every one of them. But thanks for trying. No, you see it's vital we get a good attendance. Absolutely vital. Mr Gosforth has worked tirelessly. I'm o/c teas. Tea lady for the day. I usually teach at the school.

**Mrs Pearce** Oh, how interesting.

**Milly** Quite a challenge, I can tell you. Most of the children round here are as thick as two planks. We don't seem to have any budding village genius . . .

*The sound of Gosforth's voice is heard off, through a loud-hailer, shouting "Keep off there, you boys"*

Oh, here's Mr Gosforth.

**Mrs Pearce** Ah.

*Gosforth enters. He is beery-faced, shirtsleeved, perspiring, at present a born leader of men. In one hand, he carries a battery-operated loud-hailer, in the other, a plastic carrier-bag filled with clinking bottles. He looks as if he is in the thick of battle. As soon as he has entered, he turns and glares out through the tent entrance*

**Gosforth** (*bellowing through his loud-hailer*) Will all you Wolf Cubs come down off that scaffolding at once. This is your last warning. (*Lowering the loud-hailer and turning into the tent*) Bloody little vandals, swarming all over it like . . . (*Seeing Mrs Pearce*) Ah. . .

**Milly** Mr Gosforth, this is Councillor Pearce.

**Gosforth** Oh good lord, hallo. (*He puts the loud-hailer on the table and shakes hands*)

**Mrs Pearce** How do you do.

**Gosforth** Gordon Gosforth. So nice of you to come. Sorry I wasn't there to meet you. Been having a bit of a guy-rope crisis.

**Mrs Pearce** Oh dear.

**Gosforth** We rented both these damn tents, you see. Didn't really open them up until today. Didn't have the space. When we do, we find half the guy ropes are missing off the main marquee—this one's safe enough —had to do an emergency job. Not a window left in the district with any sash cord. (*He laughs*) Now, the curriculum goes as follows. Two-thirty p.m. we plan to kick-off. I'll give you a short introduction— needn't be too long—as soon as you've finished—up strikes the band— got them coming over from Hadforth—they should be here—why aren't they?—then if you can mingle about a bit if you don't mind a spot of mingling—have a go at bowling for the pig—just seen Fred Crake's trailer so the pig's arrived safely, thank God—roll a few pennies and all that sort of thing—then, at three-thirty—if you can stay till then—I hope you can—Second Little Pendon Wolf Cubs' P.T. Display, organized by Stewart Stokes—that should go on for about half-an-hour—four o'clock tea, courtesy Milly Carter and assorted ladies—four-thirty, soon as they've swallowed their biscuits—novelty races, fathers' race, mothers' race, three-legged grandfathers' race, all that sort of rubbish—five-thirty to six—final round-off with an organized sing-song with the Hadforth Band—has the Reverend managed to get the song-sheets run off?—ten pounds to a quid he hasn't—six o'clock all pack up, dismantle tents—seven-thirty all cleared away because old Swales wants the field back for his cows first thing in the morning. Hope you can stay for a bit of the fun.

**Mrs Pearce** Yes.

**Gosforth** Sure you'll want to. Milly, where is that blasted man Fair-child?

**Milly** He said he'd be back. He had to go on a call.

**Gosforth** He had better be back. Not a solitary thing is working. (*To Mrs Pearce*) Penalty of having a local quack who is also the electrical expert. (*He indicates the amplifier*) Rigged up the entire sound system— got all the wires down—microphones—amplifier there, you see—loud-speakers, the lot. Only trouble is, not a bloody thing's working. Now he's taken off on some emergency.

**Mrs Pearce** Oh dear.

**Gosforth** Oh dear, indeed. If he doesn't fix it when you make your speech nobody'll hear a word you're saying . . .

*There is a rumble of thunder*

That sounds ominous. Milly, my darling . . .

**Milly** Yes, Gordon?

**Gosforth** (*handing her the carrier-bag*) These are some prizes for the races. Half a dozen bottles of sherry. Could you hide them behind the counter where the Cubs can't get at them. (*To Mrs Pearce*) Advantages of running a pub. Ready-made prizes always to hand. (*He catches sight of something going on outside the tent behind her*) Excuse me a minute. (*Snatching up the loud-hailer and shouting through it*) Reverend, over here. Reverend, would you mind . . . (*Lowering the loud-hailer, to Mrs Pearce*) Useful gadget this. Saves the voice. Would you like a look round before we start, Councillor Mrs Pearce? We may be a few minutes. I think you'll find it impressive. What there is of it so far, anyway.

**Mrs Pearce** Lovely.

*The Vicar enters, laughing. He laughs a lot, especially when he is nervous*

**Vicar** (*laughing*) Hallo there. Bad news, I'm afraid, Gosforth.

**Gosforth** What's happened?

**Vicar** I've been finally let down on the song-sheets, I'm afraid.

**Gosforth** (*clasping his head*) Oh—(*inaudibly*)—help us. Pardon the language.

**Vicar** No, the man who owned the duplicator has gone out of business.

**Gosforth** Oh well. Delete community singing. Insert community humming.

**Vicar** (*laughing*) Community humming, I like that . . . (*Seeing Mrs Pearce*) Oh, I beg your . . .

**Gosforth** I'm so sorry. Councillor Mrs Pearce, this is John Braithwaite, our vicar.

**Mrs Pearce** How do you do.

*They shake hands*

**Vicar** How do you do. Very kind of you—to turn out. And how is your husband? Better, I hope.

**Mrs Pearce** He's not ill.

**Vicar** Oh dear, seriously?

**Mrs Pearce** No, he's not ill.

**Vicar** Oh, I beg your pardon. I thought you said he got ill. He's not ill. That's better.

**Mrs Pearce** Yes.

**Vicar** There's a big difference between not ill and got ill, isn't there? No, we don't want to get those two confused.

**Gosforth** John, I wonder if you'd like to show Councillor Mrs Pearce the lie of the land. Take her for a turn round the tombola.

**Vicar** Of course. Delighted.

**Gosforth** If you'll excuse me, Councillor—I think I'll have to pitch in to this public address system—see what I can do with it myself.

**Mrs Pearce** Yes, of course.

**Gosforth** Twelve loudspeakers strung all the way round the field and not a squeak out of any of them.

**Vicar** Would you care to follow me, Councillor?

**Mrs Pearce** Yes, of course. See you later.

*Mrs Pearce exits*

**Gosforth** Yes indeed. And Vicar, would you tell those confounded Wolf
  Cubs to come down off that scaffolding. It was only built for loud-
  speakers, you see.
**Vicar** I will, I will.
**Gosforth** They're not designed to take that sort of weight, you see.
**Vicar** Quite. Point taken.

*The Vicar exits*

**Gosforth** In fact, as far as I can make out, they're not designed to take
  any sort of weight. Now then, how's my little Milly, all right?
**Milly** I think we're all right. Old Mr Durban is bringing the tea urn over
  in a minute.
**Gosforth** Splendid. Now then . . .

*Thunder*

  Oh, grief. Hark at that. Now then, where do I start with this lot. (*He
  looks at the amplifier on the floor*) The amplifier seems to be working
  okay. (*He turns on the light*) Well, anyway, the light's on . . .
**Milly** Gordon . . .
**Gosforth** (*involved*) Just a second, lovey . . . I'd better start at the business
  end and work round. Loose connection somewhere. That's all it can
  be. (*He starts to examine the mike plugs and lead, testing them from
  time to time*) Hallo, hallo, one, two, three, four, five.
**Milly** Gordon, have you a minute, please?
**Gosforth** Hallo, hallo. Where the hell's that damn fiancé of yours got to?
**Milly** I don't know.
**Gosforth** Well, I wish he'd stick around. He could have helped me sort
  this out. He's never around when you need him. Those damn Wolf
  Cubs of his are running amok.
**Milly** Gordon, have you got a minute? Please . . .
**Gosforth** (*sitting on a chair, still fiddling with the mike*) Darling girl, does
  it look as if I've got a minute?
**Milly** It's frightfully urgent, Gordon.
**Gosforth** All right, old girl, go ahead. I'll just keep fiddling.
**Milly** Well . . . (*She pauses*)
**Gosforth** Uh-huh . . .
**Milly** It's really rather awful. It does seem terribly as if perhaps I might be
  pregnant.
**Gosforth** Oh yes.
**Milly** Yes.

*Gosforth drops the mike, as he realizes what she has said. The jolt causes the
mike to become live. We hear, distantly, their voices echoing away on a*

*series of loudspeakers. They alone, in their concern, remain unaware of this*

**Gosforth**  Did you say pregnant?
**Milly**  I'm frightfully sorry.
**Gosforth**  Me?
**Milly**  There's no-one else it could have been, Gordon.
**Gosforth**  Oh my God. (*He rises, with the mike*)
**Milly**  I'm really awfully sorry. What are we going to do?
**Gosforth**  Well . . .
**Milly**  What am I going to say to Stewart?
**Gosforth**  Oh . . .
**Milly**  He'll be dreadfully upset
**Gosforth**  Yes, I can see he might, yes.
**Milly**  He might refuse to marry me.
**Gosforth**  Yes, I can see he might, yes.
**Milly**  (*her lip trembling*) I don't know what to do.
**Gosforth**  Now, easy, easy, Milly. (*He puts his arm round her*) Now, you're absolutely sure.
**Milly**  Yes.
**Gosforth**  Yes. Well. This needs thinking about.
**Milly**  What's Stewart going to say when he finds out? What's it going to do to him? Everyone knows we're engaged. How's he going to face his Cubs?
**Gosforth**  Well, he's a good bloke. He's a Scout, isn't he, after all. He's pretty decent. Now listen, Milly, we must just get through today first. Then we'll talk about it. You see?
**Milly**  Yes.
**Gosforth**  Don't worry.
**Milly**  No.
**Gosforth**  You're not to worry, we'll sort it out. But first things first. You get your tea organized and I'll see if I can get this wretched thing to—one, two, three—ah, success, it's working—don't know what it was I did but I—ah . . .

*They look at each other, appalled*

**Milly**  How long's it been on for?
**Gosforth**  Very good point.

*Stewart Stokes enters in full Scout kit. Normally a pink young man—he is now red with fury*

**Milly**  Stewart . . . !
**Stewart**  You bastard, Gosforth . . .
**Gosforth**  Hallo, old boy.
**Stewart**  You complete and utter bastard, Gosforth.
**Gosforth**  Now keep calm, Stokes.
**Stewart**  I'm going to kill you, Gosforth.

**Gosforth** Stokes, keep calm.

**Stewart** With my bare hands.

**Gosforth** I warn you, Stokes, this thing is live.

**Stewart** Well, switch it off, you coward, switch it off.

**Gosforth** I don't know how to switch it off.

**Stewart** Haven't you done enough? How do you think it feels to hear the news that my fiancée is pregnant by another man? Isn't that bad enough? But when you publicly announce it over four acres of field . . . in front of all my Cubs . . .

**Gosforth** I say, Stewart, I'm sorry.

**Stewart** There are Brownies out there as well, you know.

**Gosforth** This is still on, Stewart, this is still on.

*Stewart throws down his Scout's pole, seizes the mike and tries to wrest it from Gosforth's hand*

**Stewart** And turn it off! Turn it off!

**Gosforth** Steady, steady, steady. This thing is still on. Milly, turn it off. Turn it off!

**Milly** Wait, wait, stop it. (*She switches the amplifier off*) It's off now. It's off.

**Gosforth** Thank God.

**Milly** Stewart, we'll have to talk about this later.

**Stewart** I do not want to talk about this later. I do not want to talk about it at all.

**Milly** Stewart, please. It's no help to anyone getting in a state.

**Gosforth** She's quite right, Stewart old man, she's quite right.

**Stewart** (*collapsing in a chair, almost in tears*) Four acres—four acres . . .

**Gosforth** Steady, Stewart, old boy, steady. We'll sort it out, I promise. We'll all sit down later and sort it out. Milly, crack open one of those bottles of mine, would you? Give him a glass of sherry.

**Stewart** I don't drink. You know I never drink.

**Gosforth** Well, you're in need of one now. Milly . . .

**Milly** Yes, just a minute.

*Milly opens a bottle and pours some into a cup*

*The Vicar sticks his head into the tent*

**Vicar** Excuse me.

**Gosforth** Yes, Vicar?

**Vicar** Were you aware that your ill-tidings were being broadcast abroad?

**Gosforth** Yes. Thank you, John, we were aware.

**Vicar** I see. Oh dear. I'm dreadfully sorry . . .

**Gosforth** Yes. Thank you, John, thank you.

*The Vicar goes*

Oh well, sorry, Milly. There goes your reputation as spinster of this parish.

**Stewart** That's not funny, Gosforth.

**Gosforth** Sorry, old boy, sorry.

**Milly** (*bringing over the cup and bottle of sherry*) Here . . .

**Gosforth** Here we are. Drink up, old boy, drink up.

*Stewart drinks reluctantly*

**Milly** Perhaps he ought to lie down in the first-aid tent.

**Stewart** I don't want to lie down.

**Gosforth** The first-aid tent isn't up yet. Someone's swiped one of their poles.

**Stewart** I've got things I have to do.

**Milly** What?

**Stewart** I haven't finished the platform.

*It starts to rain*

**Gosforth** You haven't? Oh lord.

**Milly** What platform?

**Gosforth** The platform upon which Councillor Mrs Pearce is supposed to make her speech twenty minutes ago. We need that finished. Can't start at all otherwise.

**Milly** Well, can't someone else . . .?

**Stewart** It's all right. I'll do it, I'll do it.

**Gosforth** (*at the tent flap*) Oh no. Here comes the wretched rain.

**Milly** Oh no.

*Thunder*

Oh, just look at it. Nobody'll come and the ones that are here will go home.

**Gosforth** Dear oh dear. Like a monsoon. Hang on, I'll try raising their morale. Try and keep them here somehow. (*He snatches up the loud-hailer and stands in the doorway*) This is only a short shower. Please feel free to shelter in the main marquee. I repeat this is only a short shower. (*He lowers the loud-hailer*) I don't think that convinced anybody.

**Milly** (*suddenly*) Oh, heavens.

**Gosforth** What is it?

**Milly** I left the biscuits out the back . . .

*Millie hurries out, after picking up a newspaper to protect her hair*

*Stewart sits drinking*

**Gosforth** I wouldn't drink too much of that, Stewart old boy, if you're not used to it.

**Stewart** Go to hell, Gosforth, you fascist.

**Gosforth** Your platform's getting a bit damp out there. Want a hand to drag it in?

**Stewart** Go to hell, Gosforth, you swine.

**Gosforth** All right, I'll drag it in.

*Gosforth goes out, as Milly comes in with a cardboard box of biscuits*

**Milly** Phew! Just saved them in time. Could you give me a hand, Stewart? Stewart ...
**Stewart** Hah!
**Milly** Oh, well. Don't then ...

*Milly goes out. Gosforth comes in through the other doorway, dragging Stewart's platform. A small, square rostrum with a rail like a wayside pulpit*

**Gosforth** Pity to let this get ruined. You put a lot of effort into this. Never seen such a shower out there. The lucky-dip tub's like a water-butt already. What was there left to do on this, Stokes? Stokes? Oh, come on, stop sitting there feeling sorry for yourself, Stokes ...

*Milly staggers in with a second box of biscuits, holding the wet newspaper on her head*

**Milly** Could one of you give old Mr Durban a hand with the tea urn? He seems to have got bogged down in the mud by the gate. He's stuck.
**Gosforth** All right, all right, I'll go. No use expecting our Boy Scout to do anything.

*Gosforth goes out through the other door*

**Milly** Oh, Stewart, honestly, just sitting there leaving poor old Mr Durban to cope. He's over seventy, you know—and those Wolf Cubs of yours are throwing mud at each other. I wish you'd try and control them. They should be taking shelter. Oh well, don't blame me if they all go down with pneumonia.
**Stewart** What made you do it, Milly?
**Milly** What?
**Stewart** With a man like—Gosforth? That fascist ...
**Milly** Oh, don't drag politics into it, Stewart, for goodness' sake.
**Stewart** What made you do it, Milly?
**Milly** (*brightly*) Oh, I don't know. Can't remember now.
**Stewart** What do you mean, you can't remember?
**Milly** (*taking the newspaper from her head*) Well, I suppose I can, yes. It was while you were off at the Scout Jamboree.
**Stewart** Oh God ...
**Milly** I went across to the pub to get some brandy—for Mother—she thought she had a cold coming. She wanted some in her hot milk.
**Stewart** Go on.
**Milly** Well—Gordon was there, behind the bar as usual. It was a very quiet evening for some reason. No-one in the saloon at all. He offered to buy me a drink.
**Stewart** He got you drunk. (*He takes another swig*)

**Milly** No, he didn't. Not very, anyway. Not as drunk as you'll get if you keep going at that the way you are.

**Stewart** Typical. Got you drunk and then took advantage of you.

**Milly** Do you want to hear what happened or not?

**Stewart** No. Yes—I don't know.

**Milly** Anyway. It sort of got later—and—Mother didn't get her brandy. Gordon closed up the bar and we sat on in there talking. He told me all about his ex-wife and I talked about you.

**Stewart** You talked to him about me? Us?

**Milly** Yes.

**Stewart** How dare you talk to that man about us.

**Milly** Oh, for heaven's sake, Stewart, if you're going to be righteously indignant, do take off that stupid hat.

**Stewart** This is not a stupid hat.

**Milly** It is on you.

**Stewart** This is my badge of office.

**Milly** And those absurd baggy shorts.

**Stewart** You always said you liked me in my uniform . . .

**Milly** Well, I don't any more.

**Stewart** I don't know what's got into you, Milly.

**Milly** I don't either. I've grown up, I think. I'm thirty-four, pregnant by a man I don't much care for and I've grown up. And not before bloody time . . .

*Milly goes out*

*Stewart stands unsteadily, adjusts his uniform and pours himself another drink*

*The Vicar enters holding a notice-board over his head which reads: "Grand Fête Today 2.30 p.m." In his other hand, a microphone stand*

**Vicar** My goodness, my goodness. Ah, Stewart.

**Stewart** Hallo, Vicar.

**Vicar** You—er—heard the broadcast—I take it?

**Stewart** Yes. I did.

**Vicar** I'm sorry. Not the most tactful way to hear that sort of news.

**Stewart** No.

**Vicar** It must have come as a great shock to you.

**Stewart** To everyone. Everyone heard it, you know.

**Vicar** Ah, yes. But then everyone knew it, you see. Except you, that is.

**Stewart** They did?

**Vicar** Oh, yes.

**Stewart** How?

**Vicar** Well, it's a very small village, isn't it? And the spectacle of Miss Carter being let out at the side door of the "Fox and Hounds" at six a.m. on a Sunday morning is not all that common an occurrence.

**Stewart** I see.

**Vicar** If you hadn't been at your Jamboree, I . . . (*Holding up the mike stand*) I brought this in with me. I don't know if it's vital to anything.

**Stewart** Oh yes, it's the microphone stand, I think.

**Vicar** Ah. Well. Your Wolf Cubs appear to be rolling in the mud.

**Stewart** Let them. Who cares.

**Vicar** Well, no, they're enjoying themselves. I don't know what their mothers are going to say. All those clean white P.T. vests.

*Gosforth staggers in with the tea urn, followed by Milly*

**Milly** Can you manage?

*The Vicar goes to help, but burns his hand on it*

**Gosforth** Yes—weighs a ton . . . (*Dumping it down on the end of the table*) Right. That's it. There we are.

**Milly** It's a good job you rescued him. Old Mr Durban had sunk in up to his knees.

**Vicar** Oh dear.

**Gosforth** Well now. Change of plan is called for, I think—Stewart, will you lay off that stuff. I think in view of the weather an early tea is called for. Can you manage that, Milly?

**Milly** Yes, I think so. I've seen Mrs Winchurch around somewhere. She can help me. My other ladies weren't due till three-thirty.

**Gosforth** And what the hell's happened to the Hadforth Band? They should have been here half an hour ago. Right. Revised schedule of event one. Opening speech by Councillor Mrs Pearce . . .

**Milly** In the rain?

**Gosforth** She needn't get wet. We can put that platform in the tent entrance there—she can stand just inside the doorway. Anyway, even if they can't see her they can hear her. As soon as she's through—tea. Then we just pray that by the time we've finished that, this lot will have passed over. We'll have to scrub round the gym display—I don't think the instructor's quite up to it anyway.

**Stewart** Go to blazes, Gosforth. (*He drinks again, from the bottle*)

**Gosforth** And to you, old boy. Now then, let's—where the devil is she?

**Milly** Who?

**Gosforth** Councillor Mrs Pearce? Where is she? What did you do with her, Vicar?

**Vicar** Oh. Yes. I think I rather lost sight of her during the—broadcast. I thought she was—that's odd. Oh dear.

**Gosforth** (*snatching up his loud-hailer and marching to the door*) Councillor Mrs Pearce. Would Councillor Mrs Pearce kindly report to the tea tent. (*Lowering the loud-hailer*) She can't have got far.

**Vicar** I'll see if I can find her.

*The Vicar runs out with his notice-board over his head*

*A big clap of thunder is heard. Gosforth starts fixing the mike into its stand which he arranges in front of the platform in the doorway. Milly starts to put out a few cups and saucers*

**Milly** I wonder how many there's going to be of them?

**Gosforth** How many cups have you got there?

**Milly** About three hundred and fifty.

**Gosforth** Well, I should start with about six. (*Examining the amplifier*) My God, the rain's getting on to this thing. It'll short out completely if we're not careful. (*He moves it to the side of the table. Stewart obstructs him*) Look, Stewart, would you mind . . . Milly, will you get your boy-friend out of the road, please.

**Stewart** I'm not her boy-friend.

**Milly** He's not my boy-friend.

*The Vicar returns*

**Vicar** No sight nor sound of her. I hope she's all right.

**Gosforth** Where the hell has she got to? She can't have vanished into thin . . .

*Mrs Pearce enters through the other door. Her feather hat is limp, her shoes and stockings coated in mud. She is exhausted and soaked*

*Milly stifles a scream*

**Gosforth** Councillor Mrs Pearce!

**Vicar** Good heavens.

**Mrs Pearce** Oh. At last . . .

**Vicar** Do sit down, Mrs Pearce, please.

**Milly** What happened to you?

**Mrs Pearce** (*breathless*) I went—I saw your church—I thought I had time to take a quick look . . .

**Vicar** Yes, yes. You're very welcome to.

**Mrs Pearce** It started raining—I found I'd lost my sense of direction. One of your Wolf Cubs finally directed me . . .

**Vicar** Good boy, good boy . . .

**Mrs Pearce** The wrong way. I finished up in a ploughed field.

**Gosforth** Typical. Pack of little vandals . . . Mrs Pearce, if you're feeling up to it, I really feel we ought to start the ceremony—for what it's worth. Then we can get on with our tea.

**Mrs Pearce** All right.

**Gosforth** Feeling fit?

**Mrs Pearce** Yes, yes.

**Gosforth** Right, then. Let's get weaving. With or without the Hadforth Band, blast them. (*Switching on the amplifier*) Just pray this thing's still working.

**Stewart** You swine, Gosforth.

**Gosforth** (*ignoring Stewart*) So far so good. (*He climbs on the platform.*

*He taps the mike experimentally*) One—two—three—four—success.
Good afternoon to you, ladies and gentlemen—boys and girls. (*Breaking off as he sights something*) Will you Wolf Cubs not persecute that
pig, please. Now keep well clear of the pig—thank you. (*Resuming*) May I first of all thank you all for braving the elements this
afternoon and coming along here to support this very worthwhile
cause. That cause is, as we all know, the building of the new village
hall. Something that eventually can be enjoyed by each and everyone
of us in this community. I won't keep you longer than I have to—
I'm well aware this is hardly the weather for standing about and
listening to speeches. We will, in view of the circumstances, be altering our programme of events slightly. We plan to take tea in the
tea tent, that is the tent from which I am speaking to you now, immediately after we have heard from our distinguished Guest of
Honour. She herself needs very little introduction I am sure. Both
she and her husband have both served as councillors for this ward
for many years and during that time have, I feel—and here I'm
speaking over and above any purely party political feeling—have, I feel,
done tremendous work both for us and for that whole community
to which we all belong. Without further ado, may I call upon Councillor
Mrs Pearce formally to open this Grand Fête. Councillor Mrs Pearce.

*Gosforth steps down to make room for Mrs Pearce. Meanwhile, under this
previous speech:*

**Vicar** (*to Milly, in a whisper*) Do you think it would be very wicked of me
to sneak a cup of tea now?
**Milly** (*whispering*) Not at all. Help yourself.
**Vicar** (*whispering*) Thank you. I will.

*Milly returns her attention to the speech. The Vicar goes over and takes a
cup. Anxious not to get in anyone's way, he swivels the urn round so that the
tap is directly over the amplifier. He turns on the tap and starts to fill his
cup. Stewart, now lying on the ground, starts to sing softly*

**Milly** (*to Stewart*) Ssh.

*The Vicar, having poured his tea, finds he is unable to turn off the tap of the
tea urn*

**Vicar** Oh dear.
**Milly** Ssh.
**Vicar** Help!
**Milly** What?
**Vicar** I can't turn off the tap.
**Milly** Oh. Wait . . .

*Milly dashes over, hands him another empty cup to catch the flow and takes
the full one from him. They continue this chain of filling cups, in between
time trying vainly to stem the flow of tea from the urn without success.
This continues until Gosforth has finished his speech. As soon as he has
done so, Mrs Pearce steps on to the rostrum*

**Mrs Pearce** Ladies and gentlemen. I seem to have brought the wrong weather with me, I'm afraid. But this is an occurrence which I don't think for once you can blame on either me or the Conservative Party. It reminds me very much of a saying my husband is very fond of quoting. The rain in Spain may indeed fall mainly on the plain—but what's left of it seems to fall mainly in Kent. Joking apart, and I don't want to turn this into a political occasion in any way—but since we have been in control of your Council—I think everyone here will agree with me—the Conservatives have made startling progress—(*gripping the microphone*)—progress not only for the rich among you but also for the not so well off—not only for the rich man in his castle—but also for the poor man at his gate—if I may, I'd like to take a brief look at our recent record on Council Housing. Over three hundred new houses in less than two years. Compared, I may remind you, with the previous Labour best of only a hundred and fifty Council houses. In other words, a hundred per cent increase. Startling indeed . . .

*Under the above:*

**Gosforth** (*in an urgent whisper*) What the blazes are you doing?
**Milly** It's stuck.
**Gosforth** What's stuck?
**Milly** The tap's stuck.
**Vicar** Could we possibly turn it upside down?
**Gosforth** Why the hell don't you leave things alone?

*Stewart has found the loud-hailer and begins to croon through it, softly at first, a selection of camp-fire songs*

**Stewart** Ging gang gooly gooly gooly gooly watcha . . .
**Gosforth** Shut up, Stokes! Milly, get that off him.
**Milly** (*who is preoccupied running to and fro with cups*) How can I?
**Gosforth** (*wrestling with the tap*) Damn and blast this thing.
**Stewart** Here we sit like birds in the wilderness . . .
**Milly** Shut up, Stewart.
**Stewart** (*at Mrs Pearce*) Right-wing fascist propaganda.
**Gosforth** Stokes! Someone get him out of here.
**Stewart** Long live the Revolution!
**Gosforth** (*moving away from the urn*) Just a minute. Keep things going, keep things going . . .

*Gosforth goes to Stewart, takes the loud-hailer off him and drags him roughly to his feet*

Come on, you, come on.
**Stewart** Kindly do not molest me, you adulterer.
**Gosforth** Come on. Out in the fresh air. (*He drags Stewart to the other entrance*)
**Stewart** Baden-Powell for President.
**Gosforth** Come on.
**Stewart** Home Rule for Wolf Cubs.

*Gosforth drags Stewart out*

*Milly and the Vicar continue to drain off the urn into a growing number of cups*

**Milly** We're never going to drink all this tea.
**Vicar** Quickly, please, quickly.
**Milly** I'm being as quick as I can.

*Gosforth returns, wiping his hands*

**Gosforth** That's fixed him. Right. Next job. Now stand clear, Vicar, stand clear.
**Vicar** I don't think I should. I might . . .
**Gosforth** (*pushing him back*) Please stand clear.

*Gosforth wrestles with the tap afresh. With the Vicar's cup no longer there to catch it, the tea pours into the amplifier below. There is a loud buzzing and howling noise from the loudspeaker system. Mrs Pearce, who is holding the mike and still in full flow, suddenly begins both physically and vocally to oscillate violently. Gosforth manages to turn off the urn*

   Done it! (*Aware of the din*) What the hell's happening?
**Milly** Look . . . (*She points to Mrs Pearce*)
**Vicar** Good gracious. (*He runs to Mrs Pearce*) Mrs Pearce . . .

*The Vicar and Gosforth lever Mrs Pearce away from the mike. The Vicar grabs the stand and gets a shock*

**Gosforth** Steady, Vicar, steady . . .

*Gosforth hits the Vicar's hand from the stand, and turns in time to catch Mrs Pearce, who collapses*

   Give us a hand, Milly.
**Milly** (*going to do so*) Right.
**Gosforth** Are you all right, Councillor Mrs Pearce?
**Mrs Pearce** (*weakly quavering*) The Conservative Party have always striven . . .
**Gosforth** Vicar, can you and Milly lift her over to the first-aid people?
**Vicar** Very well, very well.
**Gosforth** I'll hold the fort here.
**Mrs Pearce** We have always believed in a fair deal for everyone . . .
**Milly** All right, Mrs Pearce.
**Gosforth** Where the hell's that bloody Hadforth Band? It's never here when you want it.

*Milly and the Vicar assist Mrs Pearce towards the other exit*

**Vicar** We'll take her to the first-aid tent.
**Milly** It's not up.
**Gosforth** Then tell them to get it up. This is an emergency.

*Milly, the Vicar and Mrs Pearce go out*

(*Surveying the scene for a second*) Oh dear God . . . (*He snatches up the loud-hailer and jumps on to the platform*) Ladies and gentlemen. Sorry about this. Just goes to show these little technical hitches can happen to the best of us. There's going to be another slight alteration in our schedule. In fifteen minutes, at three-fifteen, we'll be having the home-made cake judging competition in the main marquee, and after . . .

*There is a loud crash*

Oh my God. Now I warned you Wolf Cubs, that scaffolding was unsafe. Please stand back, everyone. Let the first-aid people through. Please stand well back . . .

*There is the sound of a brass band approaching*

Oh dear God, what a time to turn up. (*Through the loud-hailer again*) Hadforth Band! Hadforth Band! There are Wolf Cubs on the ground requiring minor medical attention—would you please be very careful where you march. I repeat, please be very careful where you are marching . . .

*He leans on the platform rail which promptly drops away. As he falls through the tent entrance, the Lights fade to a Black-out*

# A TALK IN THE PARK

*A park*

*Four park benches, separated but not too distant from each other. On one sits Beryl, a belligerent young girl at present engrossed in reading a long letter. On another sits Charles who looks what he is, a businessman dressed for the weekend. He is slowly thumbing his way through a thick report. On another sits Doreen, middle-aged, untidily dressed, feeding the birds from a bag of breadcrumbs. On the remaining bench sits Ernest, a younger man. He sits gazing into space. The birds sing. After a moment, Arthur enters. He is a bird-like man in a long mackintosh, obviously on the look-out for company. Eventually, he approaches Beryl's bench*

**Arthur** Is this seat occupied, by any chance?
**Beryl** (*shortly*) No. (*She continues to read*)
**Arthur** Great, great. (*He sits*)

*A pause. Arthur takes deep breaths and gives a few furtive glances in Beryl's direction*

Student, I see?
**Beryl** What?
**Arthur** Student, I bet. You look like a student. Always tell a student.
**Beryl** No.
**Arthur** Ah. You look like one. You're young enough to be a student. Quite young enough. That's the life, isn't it? Being a student. Not a care in the world. Sitting in the park on a day like this. In the sunshine. Rare enough we see the sun, eh? Eh? Rare.
**Beryl** Yes. (*She refuses to be drawn into conversation*)
**Arthur** Mind you, I shouldn't be here. By rights, I should be at home. That's where I should be. Inside my front door. I've got plenty of things I should be doing. The kitchen shelves to name but three. Only you sit at home on a day like today. Sunday. Nothing to do. On your own—you think to yourself, this is no good, this won't get things done—and there you are talking to yourself. You know what they say about people who talk to themselves? Eh? Eh? Yes. So I thought it's outdoors for you, else they'll come and take you away. Mind you, I'm never at a loss. I'm a very fulfilled person. I have, for example, one of the biggest collections of cigarette cards of anyone alive or dead that I know of. And you don't get that by sitting on your behind all day. But I'll let you into a secret. Do you know what it is that's the most valuable thing there is you can hope to collect? People. I'm a collector of people. I look at them, I observe them, I hear them talk, I listen to their manner

of speaking and I think, hallo, here's another one. Different. Different again. Because I'll let you into a secret. They are like fingerprints. They are never quite the same. And I've met a number in my lifetime. Quite a number. Some good, some bad, all different. But the best of them, and I'm saying this to you quite frankly and openly, the best of them are women. They are superior people. They are better people. They are cleaner people. They are kinder-hearted people. If I had a choice, I'd be a woman. Now that makes you laugh, I expect, but it's the truth. When I choose to have a conversation, I can tell you it's with a woman every time. Because a woman is one of nature's listeners. Most men I wouldn't give the time of day to. Now I expect that shocks you but it's the truth. Trouble is, I don't get to meet as many women as I'd like to. My particular line of work does not bring me into contact with them as much as I would wish. Which is a pity.

*Beryl gets up*

**Beryl** Excuse me. (*She moves off*)
**Arthur** Are you going?

*Beryl moves to Charles's bench*

**Beryl** (*to Charles*) Excuse me, is this seat taken?
**Charles** (*barely glancing up*) No. (*He moves along his bench*)
**Beryl** (*sitting*) Thanks. Sorry, only the man over there won't stop talking. I wanted to read this in peace. I couldn't concentrate. He just kept going on and on about his collections or something. I normally don't mind too much, only if you get a letter like this, you need all your concentration. You can't have people talking in your ear—especially when you're trying to decipher writing like this. He must have been stoned out of his mind when he wrote it. It wouldn't be unusual. Look at it. He wants me to come back. Some hopes. To him. He's sorry, he didn't mean to do what he did, he won't do it again I promise, etc., etc. I seem to have heard that before. It's not the first time, I can tell you. And there's no excuse for it, is there? Violence. I mean, what am I supposed to do? Keep going back to that? Every time he loses his temper he . . . I mean, there's no excuse. A fracture, you know. It was nearly a compound fracture. That's what they told me. (*Indicating her head*) Right here. You can practically see it to this day. Two X-rays. I said to him when I got home, I said, "You bastard, you know what you did to my head?" He just stands there. The way he does. "Sorry," he says, "I'm ever so sorry." I told him. I said, "You're a bastard, that's what you are. A right, uncontrolled, violent, bad-tempered bastard." You know what he said? He says, "You call me a bastard again and I'll smash your stupid face in." That's what he says. I mean, you can't have a rational, civilized discussion with a man like that, can you? He's a right bastard. My friend Jenny, she says, "You're a looney, leave him for God's sake. You're a looney." Who needs that? You tell me one person who needs that? Only where do you go? I mean, there's all my things—my personal things. All my—everything. He's

even got my bloody Post Office book. I'll finish up back there, you
wait and see. I must be out of my tiny mind. Eh. Sometimes I just
want to jump down a deep hole and forget it. Only I know that bastard'll
be waiting at the bottom. Waiting to thump the life out of me. Eh?

**Charles** Yes. Excuse me. (*He gets up*)

**Beryl** I'm sorry, I didn't mean to embarrass you.

**Charles** No, no.

**Beryl** I just had to . . .

**Charles** Quite all right. Quite all right.

*Charles moves over to Doreen*

(*To Doreen*) Nobody here, is there?

**Doreen** What?

**Charles** Nobody here?

**Doreen** Nobody where? (*She looks round*)

**Charles** Sitting here.

**Doreen** No. No.

**Charles** Sorry. Do you mind if I do? (*He sits*) I won't disturb you. Girl over
there's got boy-friend trouble. Comes and pours it all out on me—as if
I'm interested. I mean, we've all been through it at one time or another.
Why she should think I should be interested. I mean, we've all got
troubles no doubt. But we all don't sit on a bench and bore some poor
innocent stranger to death. I mean, that in my book spells S for selfish-
ness. And have you noticed that it's invariably the young? They think
we haven't been through it. Can't imagine that perhaps we were young,
too. Don't know where they think we all came from. I mean, five years
ago I had a house in the country, a charming wife, two good children,
couldn't imagine a happier family. My wife dies suddenly, my children
can't stand the place a moment longer and emigrate to Canada so I
sell the house and there I am in a flat I can hardly swing a cat in. But
I don't go round boring other people with it. That's life. I've had
twenty—no, more like twenty-five, good years. Who am I to complain
if I get a few bad ones thrown in as well. Make no mistake, I know I'm
in for some bad ones. Things are going to get worse before they get
better. Bound to. And you know an interesting thing about trouble?
I always think it's a bit like woodworm. Once you've got a dose, if
you're not careful, it starts to spread. Starts in your family and, before
you know it, it's into your business. Which explains why I'm sitting
here reading a report that's been put together so badly that I've got to
read it through on my one day off and condense it into another report
before I can even be certain whether I'm bankrupt. I mean, I don't
know if you're interested but just take a look at this page here, this is
a typical page. Can you make head or tail . . .

*Doreen gets up and moves away*

(*Muttering*) Oh, I beg your pardon.

*Doreen moves to Ernest's bench*

**Doreen** Excuse me.

**Ernest** Eh?

**Doreen** Excuse me. May I sit here for a moment? (*She sits*) The man over there has been—you know—I didn't want to make a scene but he—you know. I mean, I suppose I should call the police—but they'd never catch him. I mean, most of the police are men as well, aren't they? Between you and me, I have heard that most of the police women are as well. Men dressed up, you know. Special Duties, so called. So my ex-husband informed me. I mean, it's terrible, you can't sit in a park these days without some men—you know—I mean, I'm on a fixed income—I don't want all that. That comes from my husband. My ex-husband. He runs a pub. In the country. But I had to leave him. We got to the stage when it was either that or—you know. I love dogs, you see, and he would never—he refused, point blank. And the day came when I knew I must have a dog. It became—you know—like an obsession. So I left. I usually have my dog here with me only he's at the vet's. He's only a puppy. They had to keep him in. He's being—you know—poor little thing. He'd have seen that man off. He's a loyal little dog. He understands every word I say to him. Every word. I said to him this morning, Ginger-boy, I said—you're coming down to the vet's with me this morning to be—you know, and his little ears pricked up and his tail wagged. He knew, you see. I think dogs are more intelligent than people. They're much better company and the wonderful thing is that once you've got a little dog, you meet other people with dogs. And what I always say is that people who have dogs they're the nicest sort of people. They're the ones I know I'd get on with.

*Ernest gets up*

Have you got a dog, by any chance?

*Ernest ignores her and creeps behind the trees to Arthur*

**Ernest** (*sitting down next to Arthur*) Excuse me. Just taking refuge. Nut case over there. Bloody woman prattling on about her dog. Ought to be locked up. Thinks every man's after her. I mean, look. Look at it. After her? She'd have to pay 'em. You know the sort though, don't you? If you let her talk to you long enough, she'll talk herself into thinking you've assaulted her. Before you know it, she's screaming blue murder, you'll be carried off by the fuzz and that's your lot. Two years if you're lucky. I mean, I came out here to get away from the wife. Don't want another one just like her, do I? I mean. That's why I'm in the park. Get away from the noise. You got kids? Don't have kids. Take my tip, don't get married. Looks all right, but believe me—nothing's your own. You've paid for it all but nothing's your own. Yap, yap, yap. Want, want, want. Never satisfied. I mean, no word of a lie, I look at her some mornings and I think, blimey, I must have won last prize in a raffle. Mind you, I dare say she's thinking the same. In fact, I know she is. Certainly keeps me at a distance. Hallo, dear, put your money on the table and she's off out. Don't see her for dust. Sunday mornings, it's a race to see who can get out first. Loser keeps the baby. Well, this morning I made it first. Here I am in the quiet. Got away from the noise. You know something interesting? Most of our lives are noise, aren't they? Artificial man-made noise. But you sit out here and you can listen—and—well, there's a bit of traffic but apart from that—peace. Like my mother used to say. Shut your eyes in the country and you can hear God breathing. (*He shuts his eyes*)

**Arthur** (*leaning across to Beryl*) Hey—hey—pssst! I've got a right one here. Thinks he's listening to God breathing . . . (*He laughs*)

**Beryl** (*leaning across to Charles*) He's talking again. To me. What do you do? (*She smiles*)

**Charles** (*leaning across to Doreen*) There she goes again. What did I tell you? Chapter Two of the boyfriend saga.

**Doreen** (*leaning across to Ernest*) He's talking to me. If he does it any more, I'll call the police . . .

**Ernest** (*to Arthur*) Oh, blimey. Why doesn't she go home? Hark at her. Can you hear her? Rabbitting on . . .

*The following, final section, is played as a Round. Doreen finishes first, then Charles cuts out, followed by Beryl, Arthur, and then Ernest*

**Arthur** (*to Beryl*) Hey—hey.

*Beryl continues to ignore him*

Oh, suit yourself.

**Beryl** (*to Charles*) Psst—psst.

*Charles ignores her*

Oh, be like that.

**Charles** (*to Doreen*) I say, I say.

*Doreen ignores him*

Oh, all right, don't then . . .

**Doreen** (*to Ernest*) Excuse me, excuse me, excuse me.

*Ernest ignores her*

Oh, really.

**Ernest** (*nudging Arthur*) Oy—oy.

*Arthur ignores him*

Oh, all right, then. Don't. Don't then. Might as well talk to yourself.

*They all sit sulkily. The Lights fade to a Black-out, and—*

*the* CURTAIN *falls*

# FURNITURE AND PROPERTY LIST

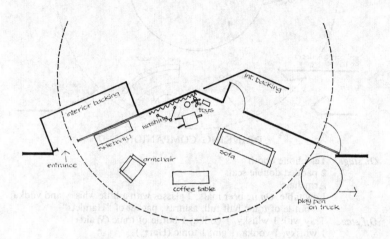

## MOTHER FIGURE

*On stage:* Sofa. *On it:* cushions, toys
Armchair. *On it:* toys, tin of baby powder, towel
Sideboard. *On it:* toys, box of tissues, telephone, lamp
Coffee-table. *On it:* toy spade. *Under it:* "Mr Poddle"
Play-pen. *In it:* toys
Airing-rack. *On it:* various articles of children's clothing
*On wall:* child's painting
*On floor:* toys, bowl of unfolded nappies

*Off stage:* Glass of water **(Lucy)**
Toilet roll **(Lucy)**
Slip of paper **(Rosemary)**
Glass of orange juice **(Lucy)**
Plate of chocolate biscuits **(Lucy)**
Glass of milk **(Lucy)**

*Personal:* **Rosemary:** key on ring

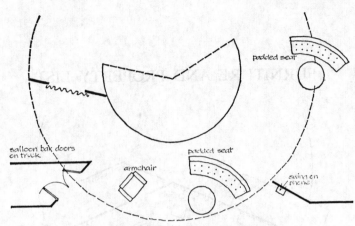

## DRINKING COMPANION

*On stage:*   Telephone booth
                2 padded double seats
                Armchair
                Low table. *On it:* beer mats, 2 glasses with a little whisky and vodka,
                    bottle of tonic half full, ashtray, packet of "Hamlets"
*Off stage:*  Tray with 1 whisky, 1 vodka, 1 bottle of tonic **(Waiter)**
                1 whisky, 1 vodka, 1 gin, 1 tonic **(Harry)**

*Personal:*   **Harry:** small change, room key 249, lighter
                **Bernice:** scent spray in handbag

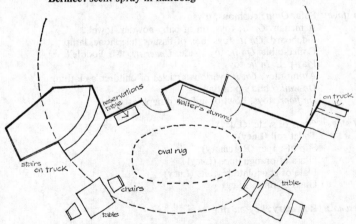

## BETWEEN MOUTHFULS

*On stage:*   4 chairs
                2 tables. *On each:* 1 white cloth, 2 knives, 2 forks, 2 side plates with
                    knives, 2 wine glasses, 2 napkins, 1 vase with flowers, cruet, book
                    matches, butter dish with butter

Waiter's dummy (serving-table). *On it:* 4 menus, 2 wine lists, 2 ash-trays, corkscrew, white cloth, tray with cutlery, steak knife, 4 fish knives and forks

Reservation table. *On it:* reservation book

*Off stage:* First Course:

| | |
|---|---|
| 1 grapefruit cocktail on small plate, spoon | |
| 1 potted shrimps, toast wrapped in napkin | |
| 1 liver pâté | |
| 1 trout | **(Waiter)** |
| 1 bottle of red wine | |
| 1 carafe of white wine | |

Second Course:

| | |
|---|---|
| 1 steak | |
| 1 Dover sole | |
| 1 vegetable dish with spoons—runner beans, carrots potatoes | |
| Lobster | **(Waiter)** |
| Chicken | |
| 1 vegetable dish as above | |

*Personal:* **Waiter:** pad, pencil, corkscrew, lighter
**Martin:** cigarettes in case
**Mrs Pearce:** cigarettes in case, lighter in handbag
**Polly:** handbag

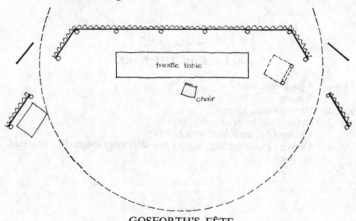

## GOSFORTH'S FÊTE

*On stage:* Long trestle table. *On it:* 2 trays of cups and saucers, tea towel, newspaper
Folding-chair
Amplifier, wired up to tape-deck. Special effect wired to prompt-corner. *On top:* microphone wired to tape-deck

*Off stage:* Box of teacups **(Milly)**
Loud-hailer **(Gosforth)**
Plastic carrier with bottles of sherry **(Gosforth)**

Cricket bat and gloves **(Vicar)**
Scout pole **(Stewart)**
2 large boxes of biscuits **(Milly)**
Small platform **(Gosforth)**
Noticeboard **(Vicar)**
Microphone stand **(Vicar)**
Tea urn, full **(Gosforth)**
Muddy clothes **(Mrs Pearce)**

*Personal:*  **Gosforth:** piece of paper with programme of events
              **Milly:** handkerchief

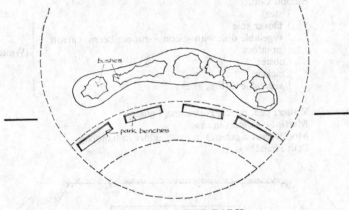

## A TALK IN THE PARK

*On stage:*  4 park benches
             Bushes
*Personal:*  **Beryl:** 3-page letter
             **Arthur:** old brown carrier-bag
             **Charles:** brown folder with report
             **Doreen:** old handbag, bag of breadcrumbs, spectacles, dog-lead in
                 pocket

# LIGHTING PLOT

## MOTHER FIGURE

Property fittings required: table lamp, wall brackets
Interior.   A sitting-room

*To open:*   Lamp and brackets on

*Cue* 1     **Lucy** replaces receiver                                    (Page 12)
            *Fade to spot on phone booth*


## DRINKING COMPANION

Property fittings required: one or two illuminated bar signs
Interior.   A bar

*To open:*   As Cue 1

*Cue* 2     As scene opens                                               (Page 13)
            *Fade up to discreet spot lighting on seats and table*

*Cue* 3     **Waiter** starts to clear empty glasses                     (Page 25)
            *Fade to Black-out*


## BETWEEN MOUTHFULS

Property fittings required: wall brackets
Interior.   A restaurant

*To open:*   Black-out

*Cue* 4     As scene opens                                               (Page 26)
            *Fade up to full, brackets on*


## GOSFORTH'S FÊTE

Property fittings required: nil
A marquee

*To open:*   General effect of dull daylight

*Cue* 5     **Gosforth:** ". . . spinster of this parish."               (Page 46)
            *Dim lighting to suggest storm*

*Cue* 6     Tea pours on amplifier                                       (Page 54)
            *Flash effect*

*Cue* 7     **Gosforth:** ". . . where you are marching . . ."           (Page 55)
            *Black-out*

## A TALK IN THE PARK

Property fittings required: nil
Exterior.   A park

*To open:*  Black-out

Cue 8        As scene opens                                              (Page 56)
             *Fade up to bright daylight*

Cue 9        **Ernest:** "Might as well talk to yourself."               (Page 60)
             *Pause, then fade to Black-out*

# EFFECTS PLOT

## MOTHER FIGURE

Cue 1    **Lucy:** "... leave Sarah alone."      **(Page 1)**
           *Telephone rings*

Cue 2    **Lucy exits to bedroom**      **(Page 1)**
           Door chimes sound twice

Cue 3    **Lucy:** "That's for Jamie's toothiepegs ..."      **(Page 1)**
           *Door chimes sound*

Cue 4    **Lucy:** "... smack your botty."      **(Page 1)**
           *Back door bell rings twice*

Cue 5    **Lucy exits to kitchen**      **(Page 4)**
           *Pause, then door chimes sound twice*

Cue 6    **Lucy:** "I'm coming ..."      **(Page 4)**
           *Door chimes sound*

Cue 7    **Lucy:** "Blooming kids. Honestly."      **(Page 12)**
           *Telephone rings*

## DRINKING COMPANION

Cue 8    **As Scene opens**      **(Page 13)**
           *Discreet Muzak*

Cue 9    **Harry:** "Very small market."      **(Page 14)**
           *Muzak fades out*

## BETWEEN MOUTHFULS

Cue 10    **As Scene opens**      **(Page 26)**
           *Discreet chatter from unseen diners—fade as action proceeds*

## GOSFORTH'S FÊTE

Cue 11    **Gosforth:** "... hear a word you're saying ..."      **(Page 42)**
           *Distant rumble of thunder*

Cue 12    **Stewart:** "... finished the platform."      **(Page 47)**
           *Rain*

Cue 13    **Milly:** "Oh no ..."      **(Page 47)**
           *Thunder*

Cue 14    **Vicar exits**      **(Page 51)**
           *Loud clap of thunder*

MADE IN GREAT BRITAIN BY
LATIMER TREND & COMPANY LTD PLYMOUTH